TALK EASY, LISTEN HARD

[
Real
Communication
for Two
Really
Different People
]

TALK EASY, LISTEN HARD

[Real Communication for Two **Really** Different People]

Nancy Sebastian Meyer

Moody Publishers
CHICAGO

© 2006 by
NANCY SEBASTIAN MEYER

Scripture taken from the *Holy Bible, New International Version®*. NIV®. Copyright © 1973, 1978, 1984 by International Bible Society. Used by permission of Zondervan Publishing House. All rights reserved.

Appendix B is adapted from *Wired That Way*, by Marita Littauer (Ventura, CA: Regal Books, Copyright 2006), 267-273. Used by permission.

Cover & Interior Design: www.DesignByJulia.com
Cover Illustration: Justine Beckett/Digital Vision/Getty Images
Editor: Ali Diaz

Library of Congress Cataloging-in-Publication Data

Meyer, Nancy Sebastian, 1961-
    Talk easy, listen hard : real communication for two really different people / Nancy Sebastian Meyer.
        p. cm.
    ISBN-13: 978-0-8024-8230-3
    1. Communication in marriage. 2. Interpersonal communication--Religious aspects--Christianity. I. Title.
BV4597.53.C64M495 2006
248.8'44--dc22

2006021209

We hope you enjoy this book from Moody Publishers. Our goal is to provide high-quality, thought-provoking books and products that connect truth to your real needs and challenges. For more information on other books and products written and produced from a biblical perspective, go to www.moodypublishers.com or write to:

Moody Publishers
820 N. LaSalle Boulevard
Chicago, IL 60610

ISBN: 0-8024-8230-9
ISBN-13: 978-0-8024-8230-3

1 3 5 7 9 10 8 6 4 2

Printed in the United States of America

TABLE OF CONTENTS

Foreword: Gary Chapman
Introduction: Why in the World Did You Say That?

Part One: Personalities—*Why We Talk*

**Part Two: Thought Continuums—
*Where Our Words Come From***

**Part Three: Love Languages—
*How We Communicate Our Feelings***

Conclusion: Okay, Now What?

Appendix A: Personal Profiles
Appendix B: Personality Questionnaire

Foreword by Gary Chapman

Communication is the name of the game when it comes to relationships. Couples may be initially attracted to each other's appearance or actions, but enduring relationships all have one common key—effective communication. That doesn't necessarily mean talking more, but talking smarter in order to make a connection.

Many of today's marriages don't pass the test of time because the two participants refuse to be the partners God designed. Both very unique individuals prize their own way of thinking and refuse to look at the situation from any other perspective (even God's). Instead of capitalizing on the differences that give the couple united strength, they can be found quarreling over petty, surface preferences, and missing the purpose and joy for which God joined them.

In fact, most couples—even husbands and wives who have been married for years—know very little about each other on matters that really count. Rarely in our me-first-my-way-I'm-in-charge-society do we hear the real truth about communication between two people: I must learn to speak the other person's language, so we can share and learn and build each other up in knowledge, wisdom, and encouragement.

To that end, I recommend to you this unique handbook that promotes real communication for two really different people. *Talk Easy, Listen Hard* is a valid approach to both biblical and psychological truths. Nancy Sebastian Meyer identifies and unwraps three facets of every individual: personality, thought continuums, and (my personal favorite) love languages. She makes these concepts simple to understand and applicable for every couple. Through the easy-to-grasp truths in this small book, she empowers men and women to learn how to effectively communicate—and thus keep love alive in relationships today.

Studying her own husband and learning to "speak his language" provided one of the keys that revitalized Nancy's relationship with her husband, Rich, during an incredibly stormy season of their marriage. Because she readily admits she's not finished learning, or applying what she already knows, I embrace the principles she shares.

Men, I encourage you to read and apply the tools that will help you focus on how your sweetheart communicates with you and why she thinks, speaks, and acts the way she does. By participating in suggested activities, honestly answering questions, and sharing together, the two of you will heighten the effectiveness of your communication and grow your love for each other.

May the Lord bless you as you continue on the never-ending, richly rewarding adventure of communication. And may your union be all God designed and desires.

INTRODUCTION
Why in the World Did You Say That?

In conversations with that special someone, do you ever think:
- What made you say *that*?
- Where did *that* come from?
- Didn't you hear anything I just said?
- You're not even listening to me!
- How did you arrive at *that* conclusion?
- Are we talking about the same thing?
- What are you *thinking*?
- That's not what I mean!

I think we've all found ourselves in those exasperating moments of disbelief—how can we be looking at the same situation totally differently? What is the other person's problem? Communication confusion is universal. Misunderstandings cross all lines of age, race, faith, sex, and marital status. In fact, almost every time I share the following story, husbands and wives tell me they can relate:

> *Stretched above the kitchen stepladder in the tiny apartment we would soon call home, I frantically called to my fiancé, "Honey! Grab this—quick!" I thought we were wallpapering together. Now where was he when I needed him?*
>
> *I watched in frustration as the gooey wallpaper slipped out of my hands, slowly pulling away from the section of wall I'd just covered. "Agh!" I glanced over my shoulder to find Rich measuring the walls. Measuring the walls! "What are you doing? Didn't you hear me?"*
>
> *His low voice rumbled, with a touch of frustration, "This kitchen is an engineering disaster." Then he turned to me and promptly looked shocked. "What are you doing with that wallpaper? We're not ready to put that up yet!"*
>
> *That's what he thought. I didn't care about the walls' perfection—or lack thereof. I wasn't rebuilding them; I was hiding them behind pretty, perky wallpaper. "Let's just stick it up so it looks right, honey," I suggested. Oh, what an exasperating man!*

Talk Easy Listen Hard

The way he glared at me left no doubt he reciprocated my feelings—toward me!

We Are So Different!

A word to the wise: you may want to hire a professional instead of trying to wallpaper with your sweetheart. That wallpaper incident almost canceled our wedding. But after twenty-some years packed with powerful lessons, Rich and I have found principles that help us relate well to each other even though we often have different ideas and approaches.

Furthermore, our relationship has taken a series of unexpected twists and turns that would have challenged two people even more similar than us. I married Rich, a youth pastor, after we graduated from Bible college together. After a bumpy ride in one church and then another, he opted out of church work and into the business world. Then just before our daughter turned a year old, Rich decided to give up on God as well—and still considers himself an agnostic. Quite remarkably and miraculously, he gives me his blessing to share our story and my faith with the world.

When our daughter, Becky, was still little, the stress of Rich's and my differences almost became our undoing. Our love for each other dropped to an all-time low, and we basically stuck to the marriage because of our promises to each other and our little girl's need for a mom and dad. Then God began stretching and convicting me, even though I thought Rich was the one with the problems. Godly people and passages of Scripture, good books and circumstances, all added up to lessons that changed *my* heart and began to restore the love in our marriage.

The words I'm sharing in this book are tried and true—based first on God's truth and then worked out in the training grounds of relationships.

So You Think I Need This Book

Stacks and stacks of marriage communication books already crowding bookshelves everywhere prove we need help. Communication is one of the most difficult, complex problems mankind faces—multiple times a day, every day, for a lifetime.

When it comes to connecting with your favorite person, are you effective? Or do you sometimes feel like one or both of you is hitting your head against a brick wall?

Bottom line: your communication, companionship, and romance will improve when you better understand each other's (1) personality, (2) thinking continuums, and (3) love languages. The unique feature of this book is that it helps you decipher all three of these and see how they are connected to each other.

Just How You Can Help Me?

If you want to climb Mount Everest you need a guide, someone trustworthy who has scaled the mountain face many times. The truths set forth in this book *work*. We've proved them a hundredfold—not only my husband and me, but other couples who have sought to love and understand each other more. Not that any of us has it all figured out. Life is a progressive journey with new lessons and experiences every day. But you and I do not travel alone. Besides the company of other sojourners, our Creator leads us on our adventure. He knows us best and loves us most, and we can trust Him to teach us and help us apply exactly what is needed for our relationships at any given moment.

Any Tips on How to Read This Book?

1. *Remember you are not alone.* Although I encourage you to read this together with your sweetheart, I realize some of you may feel like you're the only one who's making an effort. Never forget that God is with you—wanting to guide you into all truth. Even efforts you make without your partner will help you mature and have greater joy—and your relationship will certainly benefit.

2. *Journal the aha moments.* Don't gloss over this point just because you hate to journal—so do I. I live in the present, and the interruption of sitting down to write something can make me crazy.

I just want to get on to the next thought or activity. However, I'm learning the value of highlighting and jotting notes in the margins of books. Writing what I really want to remember and work on inside the back cover comes in handy when I want to review it later. Furthermore, just the act of writing down a key thought or a goal makes it more memorable. Don't forget to use the profiles in appendix A to record information about yourself and your partner as you read—directions will be given at the beginning of each of the three sections.

3. *Confess sin as God makes it known.* Sin can hide in our lives, even if we confess all known sin on a daily basis. While people often try to make us see our faults, God reveals our sin and gives us strength to change.

When you come across something God uses to convict you of sin, thank Him for revealing it. Then confess, or agree with God that it is sin, and ask His forgiveness that He grants freely because of Christ's death and resurrection (1 John 1:9). Use your new awareness to learn to avoid it in the days to come. This is Christian growth and maturity!

4. *You may feel overwhelmed.* Please read this *caution*. Sometimes we can feel crushed when our internal wiring is revealed. You may come face-to-face with a part of you that isn't pretty, a characteristic you've been trying to ignore, or a weakness you thought you'd overcome. You may even see something ugly in your partner you didn't notice before. Do not be afraid (2 Timothy 1:7). Do not give up (James 1:2–5). Nothing takes God by surprise. He's known all about the two of you since before you were born—and His love is unchanging. Take your concerns to the Father and ask Him for grace to appreciate who He created you both to be. Another thought: you don't need to fix everything right now (in fact, you can't ever *fix* another person). Only try to understand and apply what God is revealing and teaching you about you at this moment. Reading the book additional times may bring up more

opportunity to work on things God points out—later. For now, take what comes as you walk with the great Teacher. He knows you, and He loves you!

5. ***Personalize your understanding of your partner.*** People don't fit neatly into a box—everyone is unique. As you identify *general* tendencies, try not to limit your partner to one label. The more you read, the more you will begin to think you understand the other person. But the study is ongoing. Even after twenty plus years. I occasionally see something new or unexpected in my husband. So *personalize* the information you find in this book, highlighting anything that really makes sense and eliminating what doesn't fit. And continue the observation lesson "until death do us part."

6. ***Use it or lose it.*** Put one thing you're learning into practice each day. Remember books are only tools—you must *apply* the tools to see results.

7. ***Remember, God wants you to succeed!*** He created you with the ability to communicate, and He wants to help you strengthen your skills and bless others with the power of words, touch, and actions. If you are married, God has *called* you to this particular relationship with this unique person. It is true. Even if you feel like you may have picked the wrong partner, God wants you to honor your vows and love this person—and He can make the relationship a good thing! Through Christ we are sanctified, or conformed to His image. Of this process we know that: "The One who calls you is faithful and He will do it" (1 Thessalonians 5:24). Follow Him in faith to take the first steps toward knowing and loving your partner.

Sadly, I must admit that while God can change you if you allow Him to, your partner must also be willing to trust God and change in order for overarching restoration and reconciliation to occur in your marriage. But despite an unwilling spouse, if you are willing to trust and obey God, He can do amazing things in and through you—and very often bring healing to your relationship.

Okay, I'm Ready to Get Started!

To understand the concepts thoroughly, read the information at the beginning of each section: Personalities: *Why We Talk,* Thought Continuums: *Where Our Words Come From,* and Love Languages: *How We Communicate Our Feelings.* These short introductions explain how the chapters that follow fit together.

At the end of each chapter you will find *Time Together for the Two of You,* which gives you and your partner an opportunity to sit down together and discuss the concepts and information presented —as it applies to *your* relationship. Don't despair if you are reading the book alone. While you may not be able to get your partner's direct perspective, you can figure out many of the answers on your own. Remember, God is faithful to bless our obedience and equips us to persevere.

Thank you for trusting me to walk with you through this season of your life. I am praying for you as you search for the truth about yourself and your mate. May God work in your hearts to bring the two of you into a more loving, intimate, understanding relationship.

Loving God of Creation,
You know us and understand us
and You can teach us about each other.
We come before You, O Lord, with a great desire
to connect with each other in new and deeper ways
and truly understand each other's hearts.
May our relationship flourish with compassion,
forgiveness, grace, and joy
as You bless us—for our good and Your glory.
We give You thanks and praise for being
the God who goes beyond all that we can ask or imagine
according to Your power at work within
us through the Holy Spirit.
In Jesus' Name, Amen.

PART ONE

PerSONaLitieS–
WHy We TaLK

The following scenario happens almost every time Rich and I go out to eat with my parents. My dad climbs into the front passenger side of his cushy car, showing deference for Rich's love of driving. Mom and I sit in the back so we can chatter for the duration of the trip.

Pulling out of the driveway, Rich asks, "Where are we going?"

Like we never gave it a thought, Mom and I break out of our conversation for a moment. She pulls an envelope full of perfectly trimmed coupons out of her purse and proceeds to announce several good deals.

At this point I become the cheerleader for my favorite restaurants and might even recall a funny story about one of the places Mom mentioned.

Soon weary of our indecision, Rich will call for the bottom line, "So where are we going?"

Dad smiles, shrugs and says, "Doesn't really matter to me—you decide."

As obvious as it is to me now, it took me years to realize our family possesses one each of the four basic personality types. I'm an outgoing, talkative *Sanguine*. Rich is the decisive and powerful *Choleric*. My mom, with her lists and cautious nature, is very *Melancholy*. And Dad is a peace-loving *Phlegmatic*.

Because we are each complex individuals, it is wrong to use personality types to limit people with just one label. I am not completely Sanguine, nor is Rich completely Choleric. Along with my Sanguine tendencies I have some Choleric qualities, while Rich's secondary personality is Melancholy.

When I'm deciphering someone else's personality types, I generally look for clues that tell me the person has a lot of one personality (primary) and a good bit of another (secondary). A person can fall almost in the middle of two personality types— becoming a fifty-fifty mix. You may find it helpful to ask yourself, "What percentage of this primary personality fits my partner, and what percentage of this secondary personality fits?"

Personalities

Use the chart on the next page to acclimate yourself to this initial information on the four basic personality types. Most healthy personality combinations go up and down or side to side, not diagonally. For example: every personality test I took for many years came back Sanguine/Melancholy (notice their diagonal relationship on the chart). I wrestled with these opposite tendencies pulling me into many directions (spontaneous vs. planned, optimistic vs. pessimistic, loud vs. quiet, etc.). When I finally gave up my fears about being Choleric and allowed God to help those tendencies to bloom, I knew I *fit*. Ministry opportunities immediately made sense to me as God flowed through the unique wiring He created within me. My parents' role modeling had suppressed much of my Choleric tendencies, but their influence ingrained in me Melancholy organization and accountability skills that were foreign to my basic nature. How thankful I am that God is the Master Designer of our lives and has a plan to shape us through all our experiences!

> Ministry opportunities immediately made sense to me as God flowed through the unique wiring He created within me.

You may recognize the terms—Sanguine, Choleric, Melancholy, and Phlegmatic—from writings by the LaHayes and Littauers, or ancient writings by Hippocrates, the Greek philosopher who originally named the personalities. If you are acquainted with the popular DISC test, you can relate that system to what you'll find in the next four chapters (D-Choleric, I-Sanguine, S-Phlegmatic, and C-Melancholy).

It is also interesting to note that in many testing situations, the following percentages are generally true of any given test group: Choleric 3%, Sanguine 11%, Melancholy 17%, and Phlegmatic 69%. This means that in an audience of a hundred, there are very few Cholerics (doers), a handful of Sanguines (talkers), less than a fifth Melancholies (thinkers), and a whopping almost seventy percent Phlegmatics (watchers).

SANGUINE

Strengths
+ popular
+ talkative
+ dramatic
+ optimistic
+ a people-pleaser

Weaknesses
- forgetful
- lacks follow-thru
- a poor listener

Basic Desire:
FUN

CHOLERIC

Strengths
+ powerful
+ concise
+ a strong leader
+ realistic
+ results oriented

Weaknesses
- arrogant
- controlling
- brusque

Basic Desire:
CONTROL

PHLEGMATIC

Strengths
+ peaceful
+ a good listener
+ loyal
+ relaxed
+ relational

Weaknesses
- a procrastinator
- nonconfrontational
- tuned out

Basic Desire:
PEACE

MELANCHOLY

Strengths
+ perfect
+ analytical
+ sensitive
+ conscientious
+ task oriented

Weaknesses
- critical
- moody
- withdrawn

Basic Desire:
PERFECTION

Now for a few guidelines as you begin:

Guideline One:
Remember that all four personalities are equally valuable.

Guideline Two:
Think *tendencies*—be flexible within each box; don't limit.

Guideline Three:
Look for primary and secondary personalities (across or up and down).

Guideline Four:
Remember to use this as a tool, not a weapon or excuse!

Guideline Five:
Ask the Creator for revelation and correct perception.

Guideline Six:
Learning never ends—be patient with yourself and your sweetheart.

The first time I completed a personality questionnaire, Rich scored it for me. When he concluded the laborious process and glanced at the results, he took me in his arms, exclaiming, "I'm so sorry! I thought you were *trying* to annoy me all this time. It's just the way you're wired!" Perhaps your partner annoys you as much as I frustrate Rich—or visa versa. If so, these next four chapters will shed some light on why you both act the way you do and how you can learn to forgive, enjoy, and love each other the way God purposed.

As you read through the next four chapters, use the two profiles in appendix A to help you keep track of your findings. The chart is reproduced and there is a place for you to fill in a percentage beside each personality. For example, I am about 70% Sanguine, 25% Choleric, 5% Melancholy, and 0% Phlegmatic. My husband scores as 90% Choleric and 10% Melancholy.

If you fill in the profiles as you read through each of the three sections of the book, by the end you will have a comprehensive picture of yourself and your partner. The profiles will help you identify each other's inner wiring and compare your strengths and weaknesses. As you learn to appreciate one another and work together, your communication and unity will improve.

Appendix B is a personality questionnaire which you can use before, during, or after reading chapters one through four, if you feel you would like a more clinical examination of your personality. Although this might seem like a test, remember the answers are neither right nor wrong, good nor bad—the results simply indicate your preferences.

Now let's take a look at personality.

CHAPTER

tHe EFFervescent Sanguine

Sally Sanguine felt like she would burst if Steve didn't get home from work soon so she could share her amazing day. Just then she heard the garage door begin its ascent. Racing through the kitchen and into the garage, she scooted out to his car and welcomed Steve with an endless string of sentences that didn't stop even as he walked into the house and down the hallway to their bedroom. Her chatter surrounded him as he tried to escape into their adjoining bathroom, but Sally sprawled across the bed, propped her head in her hands and continued regaling him with her escapades . . .

Sound like anyone you know?

You might be Sanguine if:

HIM HER

☐ ☐ You blurt out spontaneous, instantaneous thoughts

☐ ☐ You keep life fresh and interesting for your family and friends

☐ ☐ You quickly admit mistakes and ask for forgiveness

☐ ☐ You hardly ever hold a grudge—you just don't remember, you live in the present

☐ ☐ You overflow with creative ideas that can crowd out normal responsibilities

☐ ☐ You enjoy having fun but can sometimes seem to lack significant depth

GOTTA KNOW INFO

Sanguines tend to be optimists who can drive others crazy with their irresponsibility, lack of discipline, and incessant talking. Wired with a need for fun, they also exhibit a desire to please and impress those around them. How do we figure out and tame this fun, frivolous, and sometimes frustrating personality?

Good News

Happy Sanguines can be quite charming and outgoing, great conversationalists at social events, and good at creating excitement and telling stories. They excel at motivating people to action, insuring fun for everyone, and speaking with humor and a dramatic flair. Sanguines are spontaneous, exciting, and enthusiastic—which keeps their relationships fresh. *Flexible, compromising,* and *delightful* could be additional descriptors. Generous to a fault, they can give outrageously wild gifts and freely volunteer their time and resources. In order to please you and others, they engage their playfulness and creativity. Because they often need it themselves, Sanguines are quick to forgive and show grace.

Challenging News

Sanguines are also known to be flirtatious, superficial, and inattentive. They generally lack plans and goals, don't follow through well, and fail to put down roots. They can come across as too happy or cute, tend to be poor listeners and great interrupters, and can forget almost everything you say—unless it was *their* idea.

Sanguines may be messy around the house, poor at managing money, and easily distracted from routine tasks. Despite these weaknesses and failures, they still fish around for compliments—their addiction to applause and approval can drive family and friends crazy!

Under Stress

Sanguines can be so genuinely happy and up most of the time, you definitely know when something is wrong. Depression in a Sanguine can be caused by a perceived lack of fun in life, by a sense of no hope for the future, or by feeling unloved. A troubled Sanguine often binges— overspending calories, time, money, etc. When Sanguines are down, they need attention, encouragement, and personal approval.

Biblical Bio: Peter

The apostle Peter optimistically asked Jesus if he could walk on water to Him, he impulsively cut off the ear of an arresting soldier in the Garden of Gethsemane, and he lied three times to look good to others. Headstrong Peter spoke before he thought and talked too much. Yet full of faith in his Lord and filled with the Spirit on the day of Pentecost, he became a mighty spokesperson for God, ultimately resulting in his martyrdom.

If *you* have Sanguine personality tendencies, you need to share your frustrations with your partner or someone you trust—even the simple act of talking through problems and knowing someone else cares helps tremendously.

If *your partner* is Sanguine, remember they need you to help them think through, and out of, the mess—and believe me, we Sanguines dive right off into the deep end sometimes, even if we don't know how to swim! If you're like my husband, you rationalize that you've been the rescuer enough times, and now your partner needs to learn responsibility the hard way. Just be sure to incorporate some grace into how you respond!

And sometimes the Sanguine can become depressed for no reason that makes sense to you. In their moment of panic, the best advice in the world (worldly advice, that is) comes in the form of four little magic words, uttered in a soothing tone: "It'll be okay, honey." And spiritually, praying and praising God with your Sanguine will help bring back that joyful side again.

Basic Needs

Sanguines need fun, adventure, and people! If you build a little fun into the day and plan times of recreation together you will be highly rewarded. They like to be surprised and they love to feel cherished with words of affirmation and admiration.

Remember that a Sanguine enjoys being spontaneous—*needs* to be spontaneous. A friend of mine with several children and a detailed calendar loaded with activities for every family member grumbled to me that her husband (the Sanguine) kept complaining because she "never wanted to do anything." She told him she'd be delighted to go on a date with him if they could put it on the calendar ahead of time, but he argued that putting it on the calendar would take all of the fun and excitement out of it. They resolved their problem by setting aside one "date event" every two weeks. They would alternate planning the event for each other. This meant when the husband had the opportunity to surprise and delight his wife, she could at least plan on the day and time.

Realize that Sanguines genuinely need umpteen times more verbal affirmation and encouragement than any other personality type. The compliments don't even need to be specific—just start praising and watch what happens. Override your natural impulse to wait until the person is fixed in every area and compliment what you can now! Since Sanguines thrive on praise, one positive word can motivate great things while a critical word can take the wind out of their sails. Try being positive about *anything* they are doing well, some inner quality you appreciate, or even something as trivial as how they look.

A helpful tip: Starting with the Sanguine strengths we've looked at, begin a list of your partner's general qualities and *add specific examples.* This list can serve as a reminder of the things you can be thankful for and use as compliments. Update it often, and use it even when you don't feel like praise is deserved. Remember Paul's words in Philippians 4:8: "Whatever is true, whatever is noble, whatever is right, whatever is pure, whatever is lovely, whatever is admirable—if anything is excellent or praiseworthy—think about such things."

COMBO ANYONE?

When combined with Choleric tendencies:

▶ Is an optimistic, outspoken, and influencing leader
▶ Recharges and is motivated by people
▶ Has the highest energy of all personality combinations

When combined with Phlegmatic tendencies:

▶ Is loved by everyone
▶ Is companionable and fun to be around
▶ Is easygoing, witty, and laid-back

Gotta Have It!
Needs . . .

▶ To feel loved
▶ Attention
▶ Physical affection
▶ Applause and approval for good deeds
▶ Acceptance "as is"
▶ Frequent verbal affirmation
▶ Some fun in daily experiences
▶ Hope—the anticipation that everything will be okay
▶ Someone with whom to talk out problems
▶ Accountability for self-discipline
▶ Help with organization and maintenance
▶ Help with goal setting and follow-through

THE GOD FACTOR

Because God reconciled the world to Himself through the death of His Son, the Sanguine can experience absolute and eternal acceptance and approval by God as His dearly loved child. Nothing we do can make God love us more and nothing we do can make God love us less than He does at this very moment—because His love is unconditional. We are pleasing to Him just because we are His. This knowledge has the power to free the Sanguine from the fear of rejection and brings about a desire to please God no matter what others think.

As the Sanguine learns to be still and experience a personal relationship with God (Psalm 46:10), noticeable behavioral changes occur. A mature Sanguine is motivated by love for God (2 Corinthians 5:14), is focused on the interests of *others* (Philippians 2:3–4), displays a more quiet and gentle spirit (Isaiah 32:17), becomes intentionally disciplined (Hebrews 12:11), stays the course (James 1:4), and learns to guard his or her tongue (James 3:3–16).

In addition to fortifying areas of weakness, God also brings out natural strengths He can use in His Kingdom work. A look at the lists of spiritual gifts suggests God might use Sanguines as teachers, preachers, evangelists, and encouragers (Romans 12:6–8; 1 Corinthians 12:1–31; and Ephesians 4:11). Their magnetic personality, entertaining stories, motivational delivery, enthusiasm, and talkativeness qualifies them as the mouthpiece of the Church—*when living under the control of the Holy Spirit.*

Other godly strengths naturally wired into this personality include joy and positive thinking (Philippians 4:4, 8). In the image of the Creator of the universe, the Sanguine is inventive and humorous—after all, God designed hyenas, anteaters, and other strange but wonderful living things!

Key Verse
for the Sanguine

"May the words of my mouth and the meditation of my heart be pleasing in Your sight, O Lord, my Rock and my Redeemer."

Psalm 19:14

The Sanguine reflects several aspects of God we would do well to observe and work out in our own lives. Because the Sanguine regularly makes mistakes, they are good at asking for forgiveness.

COMMUNICATION CLUES

Sanguines need personal acceptance—remember to praise personal qualities, not just actions. Personal acceptance can also be a tall order when your Sanguine is telling tall tales—they are known for exaggeration.

When Sanguines get excited about projects that make you wonder how they're going to pull everything off, they'll probably forget most of what comes out of their mouth by tomorrow—especially the really weird ideas. Be patient.

Much of the Sanguine talk is a need to "think out loud." Voicing thoughts gets them into the open where they can be processed. Having an audience motivates the Sanguine to keep on task.

Another aspect that motivates a Sanguine tongue is the desire to entertain and seek applause. Sanguines are memorable speakers and teachers due to their clever stories and crazy humor, as long as they work on organization and follow-through. They communicate well to a class of many types of learners, because they almost automatically say the same thing several times—each time in a different way. This quality drives a Choleric partner crazy, because they want the bottom line—once!

A conversation between two Sanguines can be a lively, back-and-forth affair. This is not necessarily so with another partner. Melancholies can feel like they are being driven nuts with the seemingly incessant, disconnected, and meaningless chatter!

Although it may be a difficult task, when dealing with a Sanguine, be attentive and don't tune them out. Before you become too frustrated, affirm the truth that's been spoken and ask to hear more later.

When you want to keep a Sanguine's attention, give colorful details and when possible put what you want to say into a story or illustration approach. If you need to communicate something very important that needs to be remembered, try writing it down and putting the note or list in an obvious place where the Sanguine can't miss it.

You can gauge a Sanguine's mood by the flow and pitch of their words. When excited or nervous, words come out in a torrent. Did you ever witness a nervous Sanguine embarrassing themselves and everyone around? Feelings of insecurity may cause the Sanguine to talk more than usual, too much, and often inappropriately at a time when they should definitely put a lid on it!

Consider a potential argument between partners. The Sanguine will tend to talk too much and say things that may be regretted later, and the partner with the different personality may bottle up their frustrations without saying a word. Identifying ways of dealing with conflict can help us become more aware of our need for understanding and balance. If the Sanguine can learn to put a rein on their tongue and give the other person time to collect and process thoughts before sharing, thoughtful communication can take place.

Notable Quotables

T - Is it true?
H - Is it helpful?
I - Is it inspiring?
N - Is it necessary?
K - Is it kind?

If what I am about to say does not pass those tests, I will keep my mouth shut!

ALAN REDPATH

General Communication Characteristics of a Sanguine:

‣ Uses dramatic facial expression
‣ Uses large, flamboyant gestures
‣ Often comes across as loud and boisterous
‣ Laughs easily and loudly
‣ Talks to entertain
‣ Talks to think through an idea—brainstorm
‣ Talks to anyone, anywhere, anytime
‣ Tells stories about their own disasters
‣ Talks incessantly when very upset, happy, or insecure

Talk Easy Listen Hard

For Women
Experiencing a Sanguine Man

"Honey!" Your husband's enthusiastic voice catches you by surprise in the middle of a Friday afternoon.

"I'm in the laundry room," you call, wondering why he's home early.

You hear quick footsteps coming toward you, and then, "Close your eyes. I have a surprise for you." You play along, praying this surprise won't upset the new family budget you just worked out. "Let me lead you outside." After a bumpy walk out to the front walkway, he stands behind you, making sure your eyes are still covered. Theatrically he whispers in your ear, "You (kiss, kiss) are the (kiss, kiss) proud owner (kiss, kiss) of—are you ready? (kiss, kiss)"

With a flourish, he pulls your hands away from your eyes. You are now staring at a shiny, candy apple red convertible—with the top down, of course.

"Don't you just love it? I named it 'Cherry,'" he exclaims as he walks up and down the length of the sporty car, describing every attribute. He talks up its benefits like a professional salesman. He even promises to forego his weekly coffee money to contribute to its monthly payments. "And I will personally see to its care and maintenance so it always looks this beautiful."

You resist the urge to glance toward his ever-muddy, rusty truck. Should you remind him his oil was due to be changed two weeks ago? Maybe this isn't a good time.

He escorts you to the passenger side of the car and chivalrously holds open the door. "Allow me to take you for a drive, milady." Closing your door, he saunters to the driver's side, takes the wheel, and whisks you into the sunset.

Fifteen minutes later your husband wheels back into the driveway. As he puts the car in Park, he turns to you in anticipation. "Well, honey, what do you think?" Your Sanguine husband's self-esteem hangs in the balance.

You realize that while you can't approve his gift, you do need to approve *him*. So you grin and say, "Nobody sweeps me off my feet like you do, dear. I appreciate your generous heart, your spontaneity, and your desire to make my life fun." You pat the dashboard of the car. "I haven't had this much fun on a car ride for as long as I can remember." You smile tenderly at him. "I love you."

He grins back rather sheepishly and says, "Guess I am a bit impulsive. Would it help if I told you the dealership lent it to me for a test drive—we don't have to buy it."

You breathe a sigh of relief. "You *are* impulsive, dear, but that's one of the things that keeps our marriage exciting. Maybe we should take the car back until we can afford a new one—and then I'd love to go along to pick it out."

"When I get back, can I take you out for dinner?" He strikes a gallant pose as he awaits your reply.

"Why I'd be delighted to go out to eat with my favorite person in all the world."

What makes my Sanguine guy tick?

A man with a strong Sanguine personality may seem like he's never really grown up. He enjoys having fun and impressing those around him. He's most likely a ham in front of the camera. And he's the best (and most lengthy) storyteller you've ever met!

If you look back at the past week or so and analyze your guy's behavior, you may find that the times when he was most productive were when an element of fun was present in those situations. Likewise, when a project was all grunt work with no potential for play, it probably discouraged him and drained his energy and vitality.

The Sanguine often works as a salesman, performer, politician, or in some other up-front, impressive, influential role. If this person can just keep organized and follow up on details, he will be an amazing success story. On the flip side, obligations and responsibilities—especially dull, repetitive work—can overwhelm this spontaneous, fun-loving guy. A word to the wise woman: he is highly motivated by your compliments, praise, and affirmation. He is also motivated by variety and spontaneity in the things you do together!

Stress relief for a male Sanguine can take many shapes. He might enjoy hanging out with the boys. He might be recharged by shopping for tools, sports equipment, or clothes. He might even use food, drink, and dessert to cheer up and reward himself. Watch out for binges—as an all-or-nothing type person, he's not known for control.

How do I get him to slow down and listen to me?

Most valuable communication will begin if you tell some things you appreciate about the person. Then let him know you *seriously* want to share something and need him to be quiet, listen, and give you some feedback. You may need to get in his face—literally, hands on face, encouraging eye-to-eye connection.

Then give an overview—tell what you're going to talk about and be sure he is mentally tracking with you. And be sure to offer thanks for listening after you've shared.

FOR MEN
Experiencing the Sanguine Woman

She hops in the car, out of breath from rushing around at the last minute, and you back out of the driveway. "Sorry (pant, pant) I'm (pant, pant) late."

Before you can add "again," her cell phone sings that ridiculous Camptown Races tune.

She grabs her phone, flips it open, and says, "Hello?" Pause. "No, problem, Carol, we're on our way now." Another pause. "Sure, no problem. I can handle two-and-threes this morning. Relax! Hey, how did Megan's party go?" Pause. "That's great. I've just got to tell you the ideas I came up with for my honey's big four-O!" She sends a dramatic wink in your direction. "We're here now. Gotta run. See ya soon."

She flips the phone shut and slides it into her purse and pulls the visor down to check her makeup. "Can you let me off at the kids' door? Come to think of it—can you pick me up there when

b

you're ready to leave? I think I promised to sit in with the junior church kids today." She flashes you a cute little smile. "Please?"

As you maneuver the car around other vehicles in the parking lot, you ask, "Who is going to help me greet everyone at Sunday school today—do you remember you signed us up to be the hospitality team this week?" You stop the car and look at her.

She's got her door open already. "Somebody will show up to help you, handsome!" Small pause and a little frown. "I'm sorry."

Her "thanks" seems to get caught in the door as she slams it behind her. Then the whirlwind is gone, and you're left in the dust. You've gotten tired just watching her spin into action.

After church, you pull the car around to the door to the children's area of the church. Fifteen minutes later, when few cars remain in the parking lot, you finally see your wife.

"Thanks, hon," she says as she climbs into the car less energetically than when she got out earlier in the morning. She leans over and kisses your cheek. You catch a whiff of animal crackers and glue.

You grin as you pick a piece of *something* out of her hair. "So, how was your crazy morning? Did all the little ruffians behave?" She looks exhausted. Her cell phone begins to sing. You intercept it, saying, "Let it take a message." You turn it off and slip it back in her bag. "I'm taking you home for a snooze."

She pats your hand, leans her head back against the headrest, and falls asleep shortly after.

On the way home, you rehearse the things you love about her and thank God for each one. Then you chuckle as you remember the couple who greeted *you* in Sunday school this morning—the ones who thought this was their week to shake hands with everyone.

What makes my Sanguine sweetie tick?

A wife with a strong Sanguine personality may appear to be overcommitted to high-profile projects and overly consumed with other people's needs and opinions. Her high energy level allows her to accomplish an unbelievable amount of work if she is correctly motivated.

There is also a need for fun that causes her to act silly, spontaneously shop for frivolous things, and plan parties just to entertain large groups of people (the more, the merrier). The Sanguine wife is most energized when there is an element of fun within the situation.

If you look back at the past week or so and analyze your partner's behavior, you will probably find many instances where she's helped others, talked people through problems, and added special touches that endear her to folks. You may find that the times when your wife seemed the happiest were when she was doing things for other people—and that includes you. She loves to please people.

Stress relief for a female Sanguine can take the form of shopping, partying with friends, talking on the phone, or eating to help herself feel better. Entrusting the checkbook to a Sanguine wife can be disastrous. Watch out for binges—as an all-or-nothing type person, she's not known for control.

How do I get her to shut up?

A Sanguine woman loves to talk, talks to process her thoughts, and talks to ask you questions about you too. The key to conversing with a Sanguine is interrupting her and going back and forth in a give-and-take brainstorming session. She will love you for it!

If she's not listening to you, and you've already tried the interrupting trick, gently take her face in your hands, establish eye contact, and then with a finger on her lips to silence them, tell her how much you love her and how very badly you need her to listen.

BOTTOM LINE
Goals for the Sanguine:

▶ Revel in God's acceptance and approval—and focus on pleasing *Him*
▶ Utilize strengths such as creativity, faith, hope, and presentation skills
▶ Learn skills to compensate for areas of weakness such as poor memory and disorganization

- Discipline your tongue and life for God's glory and the good of others
- Slow down, tone down, and listen up
- Include others in the spotlight and conversation
- Enjoy your unique ability to brighten people's lives

Tips for the Person Relating to the Sanguine:

- List your Sanguine's strengths and thank God for them
- Freely and regularly give affection, verbal recognition, and acceptance
- Make opportunities often for fun and spontaneity
- Reduce expectations regarding areas of discipline and organization
- Give reminders, lists, and help with follow-through
- Pray for patience to be attentive and grace for mistakes
- If frustrated ask them to share more later
- Enjoy your Sanguine!

Praying for My Sanguine

Thank You for _____ who makes my life incredibly fresh and interesting, who astounds me with creative ideas, and helps me see the positive side of things. *Help me remember* to be patient, affirming, and vocal with praise and approval.

Time Together for the Two of You

These questions are specifically designed for a couple in which one person or both people exhibit Sanguine qualities (if neither of you tends to be Sanguine, skip to the next chapter). If your partner is unwilling or unable to work with you, partner with God as you work through the following questions and ideas.

1. Which one of you has Sanguine tendencies and to what degree (**1**—not much at all–**10**—could be a poster child)?

2. Brainstorm a list of strengths the Sanguine brings to your relationship.

3. (For this question, the Sanguine should try very hard not to talk, allowing their partner adequate time to think and respond.) How does it make you (the non-Sanguine) feel when your partner interrupts you, does not allow you sufficient time to answer a question, and/or seems to disregard what you bring to the conversation, going on with their own thoughts?

4. Look back at the Bottom Line tips. Have the Sanguine partner look over the list and say which items would be especially appreciated from the other person.

5. Discuss whether your Sanguine is nearly purebred or mixed with Choleric or Phlegmatic tendencies—and how that makes them unique.

6. End your time together by having the non-Sanguine partner pray, thanking God for the specific Sanguine strengths He fearfully and wonderfully created within the other person.

The Effervescent Sanguine

CHAPTER

tHe Strategic CHOLeric

Curt Choleric fumed with frustration. "Go already, will ya?" he yelled at the elderly driver between him and the yellow traffic light. In a sarcastic tone, he added, "Oh, good. We can be late again. Thank you very much!" He could feel Cheri recoil as she sat next to him, fingers tapping nervously on the armrest of the passenger door. They were going to be late for the party he didn't even want to attend, and it was just as much his wife's fault as the car ahead of them. She was never ready on time. He glared at Cheri, who turned to look out the window . . .

Sound like anyone you know?

You might be Choleric if:

HIM HER

☐ ☐ You generally feel confident and in control

☐ ☐ You are goal oriented and accomplishment driven

☐ ☐ You enjoy a good debate

☐ ☐ You make decisions easily and quickly, relishing the risk

☐ ☐ You speak quickly, concisely and get to the bottom line

☐ ☐ You don't like to be told what to do

GOTTA KNOW INFO

Cholerics are decisive risk-takers, born to be leaders and vision-aries. On the other hand, compassion and sensitivity are not likely strong suits of this take-charge personality. How can you pass muster and earn the right to be heard by the Choleric?

Good News

Cholerics work hard, quickly, and productively. They radiate a confidence that can make family, friends, and coworkers feel invincible, energized, and protected. They motivate others to action, providing a great example by working harder than anyone else on their team. They thrive on goal setting, giving quick and clear directions, and making sure everyone sees the immediate gain.

These realists are undaunted by challenges, decisions, and responsibilities. They are driven to action, driven to accomplish, and driven to administrate plans and dreams. If you have a problem, they have a solution and will get in there and work it out with you. They are dependable, loyal, and focused on the task at hand.

Challenging News

Shortly after you get to know a Choleric, you may notice he or she has significant relationship problems. Cholerics know how to do almost anything (if not, they still give it a try), but they don't always understand the value of just sitting and talking for the sake of connection and intimacy. A Choleric husband may hardly ever

?

Talk Easy Listen Hard

tell his wife he loves her because he said it at the altar, meant it, and will stand by it—*done deal.*

Cholerics are task oriented to the extreme, focusing on projects rather than people. They can seem obsessed with power and control, almost dictatorial. They can manipulate to get their way, rationalizing the need to accomplish what they think is important. These workaholics can be obsessed with accomplishment, competition, and the need to conquer.

Under Stress

For Cholerics, disappointments are caused by other people. And these other people must be punished so they learn from their mistakes—from the inefficient waitress who gets a penny tip to the ignorant driver who forgets the rules of the road and receives a verbal dressing down (even if they can't hear it from the car behind them).

Since *control* is key, a lack of control (someone else in authority or a situation outside the Choleric's control) pushes them to depression—in the form of anger. Problems with money, health, family, or a feeling of being unappreciated will push the Choleric to work harder, exercise more, avoid unyielding situations, and become bossy toward others.

Biblical Bio: Paul

Saul, a zealous, legalistic perse- cutor of the church, was rendered helplessly blind in an encounter with God on the road to Damascus. That turning point led him to become Paul the apostle— a zealous, passionate leader who fought valiantly for the cause of Christ. He used his concise, quick tongue to proclaim the gospel and his bold, risk-taking nature to travel to unknown lands and win souls.

Basic Needs

When Cholerics are sick, they generally want to hide under their rock until they feel human again. When they hurt emotionally, they need loyalty from the troops, including specific recognition for accomplishments and appreciation.

They need to feel in control of at least *some* areas of life at all times. Because they are naturally strong and capable leaders, they want to be in charge and be recognized and treated as such by the significant people in their lives. Where Sanguines need a great deal of praise, Cholerics need specific, sincere, and timely praise. Don't be too general. And don't try to jolly up a Choleric stewing in their troubles.

COMBO ANYONE?

When combined with Sanguine tendencies:

- Is a fireball of passionate energy
- Accomplishes amazing amounts of work
- Inspires loyalty and actively motivates the troops

When combined with Melancholy tendencies:

- Quickly makes decisions and is almost always correct
- Is goal oriented and works methodically to the desired end
- Is task oriented with little interest in cultivating relationships

Gotta Have It!
Needs . . .

- A sense of control
- Loyalty from family, friends, and coworkers
- Specific recognition and appreciation for accomplishments
- Credit for good works
- Choices (don't tell them what to do; if you must, give choices)
- The bottom line *first*
- Brief and to-the-point conversation
- Compliments pertaining to any positive leadership demonstrated
- Appreciation for their strong work ethic
- Assertiveness when the tone gets verbally abusive (they don't need a doormat)
- A partner who refuses to argue—it takes two!

THE GOD FACTOR

Think for a moment about great leaders of ages past. God created, raised up, and equipped mighty men and women throughout history to do His work—Moses, Deborah, Paul, Martin Luther, Billy

Graham. We ordinary people need driven, strong, visionary Cholerics to lead, protect, plan, and take us where no man has gone.

The unique problem for a Choleric is this: God daily asks His children to hand over control of their lives to Him. God is sovereign —in control of every detail of life, but not controlling (Jeremiah 29:11; Psalm 139:16). To the Choleric, however, God can seem like another authority figure trying to tell him what to do. Yet a Choleric who yields to God gains access to divine perspective, holy strategy, and the very power of God. Cholerics are major players in Kingdom plans.

A second unique problem hampers the Choleric's search for God. By its very nature, Christianity is a relationship. The world's most eternally significant matter was performed on the cross, and Jesus said, "It is finished" (John 19:30). When the innately task-oriented Choleric finally learns how to relate to God on a personal level, then their actions will result from love for God and be performed with God. However, a Choleric Christian may do all the right things for God instead of out of *relationship with* God—and become burnt out and disillusioned.

Key Verse
for the Choleric

"But by the grace of God I am what I am, and His grace to me was not without effect. No, I worked harder than all of them —yet not I, but the grace of God that was with me."

1 Corinthians 15:10

Just imagine a Choleric filled with the Spirit of God and exhibiting, along with natural leadership skills, the spiritual fruit of kindness, compassion, patience, and gentleness! God can enable this person to lighten up, slow down, and focus attention on people. Surely this is what 1 Corinthians 13:5 means when it says about love, "It is not rude, it is not self-seeking, it is not easily angered, it keeps no record of wrongs." God can bring this about in the lives of Cholerics and make them tenderhearted and forgiving (Ephesians 4:32), as well as sympathetic, loving toward others, and humble (1 Peter 3:8).

God often uses naturally strong, fearless Cholerics in positions needing vision and leadership such as church planting, tribal missions work, and evangelism. Willing to go above and beyond, they also naturally possess discernment, wisdom, and honesty. Fair and just, they can act as true peacemakers, identifying a problem, fearlessly bring it to light, and offering a wise solution. We can admire their devotion, energy, and passion for the Lord's work.

COMMUNICATION CLUES

The best communication advice I've ever received regarding my Choleric husband came from friend and counselor Joyce Hulgus in the form of two phrases:

1. *Keep it lean and brief.*
2. *Truth resonates.*

Note that the Choleric wants the bottom line. If you take too long to get to the point, then you lose, aggravate, or anger them. With intense issues, pray and think about what you want to say ahead of time. Pare it down to the bare bones—just the meat of your message. Then speak the truth, and get off of it quickly. All truth is God's truth, and it never returns void (Isaiah 55:11). When truth resonates in the inner person, God can use His Spirit to change the heart and mind. Keep praying, of course, but learn to hold your tongue and allow God to activate real change.

Note that Cholerics are honest to a fault—but not always tactful. They understand the idea of speaking the truth, but do not necessarily do so with loving compassion (Ephesians 4:15). Because they live by "thou shalt not lie," it follows that they are turned off by deceit, lying, exaggerating, embellishing stories, and partial truth that tries to save face.

Communication is more than how you speak to the other person; it is also about how you listen and interpret what they are saying to you. This is particularly true with the Choleric, who can seem harsh and commanding, unless you realize they are focused on the task and not deliberately belittling you.

Talk Easy Listen Hard

General Communication Characteristics of a Choleric:

- Points, pounds, or wags finger
- Hands on hips
- Confident; sometimes coming across as arrogant
- Concise
- Gives quick orders
- Cuts others off—finishes their thoughts
- Dismissive of others; impatient

FOR WOMEN
Experiencing a Choleric Man

"Hey, what are you working on?" You've found your husband digging through the tools on his workshop tabletop. "Can I help?"

"Yeah, sure. I'm looking for . . . " he opens a cabinet and growls when he can't find whatever is eluding him. He bangs the door shut with frustration and turns to you. "Run up and grab my wrench from the garage—quick. Meet me in the bathroom."

"But . . . "

"Go!" He points you in the direction of the garage as he follows upstairs from the basement and then trudges off toward the bathroom.

You head to the garage hoping you will miraculously know the wrench when you see it. Could that be it? You pick through a collection of tools that make you wish you'd paid more attention the last time you "helped"—not that your husband ever really seems to appreciate your efforts.

Grabbing what looks like it might be a wrench, you trot back into the house and down the hall to the bathroom. Grumbling coming from the room doesn't bode well for you and the perceived wrench.

"No! That's not a wrench. A wrench looks like this (he draws a shape in the air). Go! I need it now!"

You hurry back to the garage with the offensive tool, keeping your mind focused on his description. Aha! There is the wrench. You relax and then remind yourself to hurry it back to him.

"Lovely." He takes the tool, tightens something and untangles himself from what looks like a terribly awkward and uncomfortable position. "All done." He straightens up and smiles.

You suddenly think how much it would have cost to hire a plumber. "Thank you for fixing this. You're so good at doing things around the house, and you're willing to try your hand at anything. I appreciate how well you take care of us and our stuff!" Your specific words of praise turn this formidable man into a teddy bear—just look at him smile!

What makes my Choleric *guy* tick?

This Choleric quickly decided you were his destiny, cut to the chase, and confidently campaigned until he won your hand. His strength of character made the woman in you feel delightfully feminine. And the less he said, the more your imagination filled in the silence with romantic thoughts you *wanted* to be filling his head. In reality, however, he is not naturally geared toward being tender, romantic, and feelings oriented.

With a strong Choleric personality, he may at times come across as arrogant, unfeeling, and even obsessed with power. He can seem manipulative, impulsive, and controlling. Where he once epitomized a protective knight in shining armor, he now seems to have forgotten you and found other dragons to slay, battles to win, and worlds to conquer. In fact, without any challenge in his life, he is one unhappy camper.

> On the **Lighter** Side
>
> A wife was overheard complaining to another woman, "I knew I married 'Mr. Right.' I just didn't know his first name was 'Always.'"

The Choleric often works as an administrator, consultant, politician or in some other role that requires risk taking, quick thinking, and innate confidence. If this person can develop people skills or grows up with a mother who teaches him manners and the value of relationships, he will be an amazing success story. On the flip side, if his brusque and arrogant manner are not addressed, both he and those around him will be miserable. A word of encouragement for his friends: remember his frustration is seldom personal.

Stress relief for a male Choleric generally takes the shape of working harder, exercising more or staying away from unyielding situations. Choleric depression looks different than that of any other personality type—extreme frustration for the Choleric most often results in anger and withdrawal.

How do I get him to see me as a person, not a project?

To get through on a personal level, pray first and think about how you can present yourself so your Choleric will give you time and attention. Remember that he appreciates honest, straightforward communication about facts more so than feelings.

If your guy wants activity, plan something for the two of you to do together that allows time for talking (movies and watching television are out). Rich and I go for long Jeep rides out in the country. As long as the top isn't down making conversation impossible, we usually talk about an assortment of topics and come home feeling more connected.

He is sure to respect you more if you notice and verbally credit him with the things he does to make your life more enjoyable. Begin making a list of his strengths and positive things to appreciate.

FOR MEN
Experiencing the Choleric Woman

Late again. She probably got stuck late at the office. You head out to the kitchen to see what you can whip up for supper. Should you make one or two portions? You pull out the egg carton and begin cracking eggs into a pan.

Okay, you're trying not to be resentful about all the time she spends on the job. She brings in a lot more money than you do—speaking of which, that also makes you a little uncomfortable. But what are you going to do about it? Complain about the extra extravagances you enjoy like the membership at the golf club and the cruise the two of you took a few months ago?

But you wonder, is it worth it? What you wouldn't give to come home to the wonderful smells of meat in the oven, a set table, and homemade dessert! Or even better, wouldn't it be great to curl up together on the couch in front of a good movie?

You hear her car and add another couple of eggs to the pan, along with a little cheese and some salt and pepper. Putting the lid on, you look up as she walks in the door. "Hi, hon."

She drops her briefcase by the door and slips out of her coat. Coming into the kitchen, she takes a deep breath and sighs, putting her arms around your waist. "It smells heavenly in here." Resting her head on your shoulder she amazes you by saying, "I don't know any other man who could be as supportive as you are with me. Thank you for making dinner when I don't get home on time and never seeming flustered by what I do—or *don't* do—around here."

You give her a hug and kiss and suggest eating dinner in front of the fire while you watch an old movie. She agrees, but you know she'll fall asleep before it's over—she always does. She works hard and then sleeps like the dead. Oh, well—better enjoy a few minutes together before she zones out.

What makes my Choleric woman tick?

A Choleric woman (especially if mixed with Sanguine) is nonstop energy. She's a driven woman—she loves to accomplish, compete, and conquer. Unless she grew up in a home that taught manners, she may issue commands and give orders without the cushion of please and thank you. You may even feel like *she's* the head of the home—a choleric woman can be bossy. In her attempt to quickly accomplish goals and tasks, she can become dismissive, arrogant, and rude. But when she turns her energies toward you and makes your home and relationship more vibrant—*wow!*

If you look at your partner's accomplishments, you will probably find many instances where she's solved difficult problems, negotiated high-level deals, and rallied her troops to do above and beyond the realm of possibility. Feeling threatened or resentful of her success are possible and dangerous responses on your part. Beyond dealing with your own emotions, if you refuse to acknowledge and forget to appreciate her accomplishments, she will pull further away and into her work. On the other hand, if you let her know you are proud of her, you will grow closer and more intimate with each other.

Let's talk control for a moment. The odd thing about control is that when you are losing it, you try to hold on tighter and ultimately make the situation worse. This happens with your Choleric woman. If a situation gets the best of her, be aware that she may tighten her control in other areas to make herself feel better. This means if she's lost a business contract at work, she may be overbearing at home. Try to be understanding—this too shall pass.

Stress relief for a female Choleric can take the form of more work, more exercise, and sometimes anger. Give her space and the benefit of the doubt —and she will soon be back to normal. In an extended time of frustration, depression can set in. Depression for Cholerics doesn't look like normal sadness and lethargy. Instead, the Choleric withdraws, shuts down, and bides her time until the situation improves and she can get back in the action.

How do I get her to slow down and lighten up?

Since opposites attract, your high energy Choleric sweetheart may be tiring you out while God naturally wired you with a lower energy base. Neither of you is right or wrong, better or worse—just different. Be yourself, and allow her the freedom to be the person God designed. There is no rule that states the two of you must do everything together, so give her your blessing to go out and do things with her friends when you just want to stay home.

To help her focus on your relationship, make sure the two of you schedule time together. Remember she likes to be active, so plan at least some of your time doing active things that allow for conversation. This counts out shopping, which can become a task, and activities like downhill skiing that she can make into a competitive event. Try boating, hiking, going out to eat, and other activities that allow you to get out of the house and do something together while you relate to each other.

BOTTOM LINE
Goals for the Choleric:

- Learn to value people, and intentionally build relationship skills
- Realize others might be right or at least have a worthwhile idea
- Learn to compromise and cooperate with others
- Slow down and lighten up; learn how to relax
- Actively listen to others and use good manners (with *please* and *thank you*)
- Schedule time to meaningfully relate to God
- Stay put—don't pace or leave

Tips for the Person Relating to the Choleric:

- Recognize the competitive, aggressive nature is natural and can be good
- Keep communication short and to the point; give the bottom line
- Don't try to fix the Choleric—your efforts will be resented
- Calmly voice when something is rude or hurts
- Back off and live the truth
- Give specific appreciation for accomplishments and service
- Generously allow them the last word when possible
- Plan things to do together that give you the opportunity to converse
- Don't always expect gentleness, patience, and kindness
- Appreciate their honesty, hard work, and dependability

Praying for My Choleric

Thank You for _____'s decisiveness, dependability and straight-forward truthfulness. *Help me remember* not to take _____'s words personally, but appreciate how much gets accomplished. Help me also remember to speak lean and brief, and live truthfully.

TIME TOGETHER FOR THE TWO OF YOU

These questions are specifically designed for a couple in which one person or both people exhibit Choleric qualities (if neither of you tend to be Choleric, skip to the next chapter). If your partner is unwilling or unable to work with you, partner with God as you work through the following questions and ideas.

1. Which one of you has Choleric tendencies and to what degree (**1**—not much at all–**10**—could be a poster child)?

2. Brainstorm a list of strengths the Choleric brings to your relationship.

3. Take turns sharing what relationship means to both of you.

4. Look at the Bottom Line tips. Have the Choleric partner look over the list and identify specific items that would be especially appreciated from the other person.

5. Discuss whether your Choleric is mostly purebred or mixed with Sanguine or Melancholy—and how that makes them unique.

6. End your time together by having the non-Choleric partner pray, thanking God for the specific Choleric strengths that God fearfully and wonderfully created within that special person.

The Strategic Choleric

CHAPTER

3

tHe ANaLyticaL MeLaNCHOLy

Melanie Melancholy frowned at her reflection in the hall mirror.

"You'll give yourself wrinkles if you keep that up!" Her husband held her coat as she put it on. Naturally jovial, he regularly teased and tried to cajole her out of her mopey moods.

Melanie ignored his comment and asked pointedly, "Did you lock the back door and turn off the light in the kitchen?"

"No, I forgot again." Mike wiggled his eyebrows comically, then sobered up. "Do you really think I need to be reminded, Mom?"

Melanie justified, "But I found the door unlocked and the lights on when I got home from the store the other day after you went to work." She walked through the door he held open for her and said over her shoulder, "I just want to take every precaution."

"You always do, dear." He opened her car door. "Did you remember our hostess gift?"

Melanie's shoulders slumped. "No." She had the deer-in-headlights look. "I'll be right back."

Mike was shocked. Melanie never forgot anything. He recovered quickly and tried to stop her with, "Relax, I'll get it." But Melanie was already scolding herself all the way back into the house.

Sound like anyone you know?

You might be Melancholy if:

HIM HER

☐ ☐ You try to be as perfect as possible

☐ ☐ You expect others to do everything the right way

☐ ☐ You like to know what's expected at the beginning of a project or event

☐ ☐ You need time, space, and silence to process your thoughts

☐ ☐ You would like to have a place for everything and everything in its place

☐ ☐ You are sensitive to details and feelings that other people often miss

GOTTA KNOW INFO

Melancholies are wired to be cautious, careful, and correct. They aim high, making it their business to know what is expected and perform it to the letter of the law. Quite frequently they drive others crazy with their negative comments and desire for perfection.

Good News

When teaching personality information, I often joke with my audience that I want a Melancholy pharmacist—someone who will fill my prescription perfectly. I don't want some optimistic, spontaneous, over-eager Sanguine to add a little of the purple stuff for color, a little of the good tasting grape stuff, and whatever they put in Aunt Maude's medicine that made her feel better so quickly! No, the Melancholy will fill the order, check, and recheck it for accuracy before handing it over.

Biblical Bio: Luke

In addition to being scrumptiously careful with every detail, Melancholies are deep, analytical thinkers. In this camp you'll also find creative artists and musicians and accurate accountants and administrative assistants—driven by a need for order.

Dr. Luke wrote the Bible books of Luke and Acts. You don't read much about him because he stayed very much in the back-ground, quietly and carefully observing what he heard about Jesus and the newly established Christian church. Can't you just see him digging a piece of parch-ment out of his robe and taking notes as Paul spoke to the crowds?

Try This. Try making praise a part of your everyday relationship. Set aside a specific time of the day or week when you can sit down together and take turns in prayer, praising God for who He is and what He is doing in the world around you. Keep each sentence short and positive—and take turns. Go back and forth until you've praised God for at least twenty things (that's just ten apiece). You'll be amazed at the joy this produces in your life and relationship.

Challenging News

Melancholies tend to shut down during con-frontation or any time they feel threatened. They rarely share freely or brainstorm with others—mostly for fear of being wrong or saying something incorrect. If they sense the other party will reject or misunderstand what they have to share, they will not offer their opinion. They don't like being wrong or having their carefully concluded ideas challenged.

The word *change* also brings turmoil to the Melancholy's world. It threatens the carefully planned and executed world of the Melancholy. Resistant to change, they withdraw from people to sort through the situation and modify expectations. During this time, the Melancholy is likely to become moody, negative, critical, and quiet, often adopting a martyr-complex.

The Analytical Melancholy

Under Stress

In the instances that Melancholies fail and disappoint themselves, they can slide into deep depression. When others fail them or life shows itself again to be very imperfect, they withdraw from people to read, study, meditate, or pray. In times of severe discouragement, they may hide in bed—or in the bottle. They feel as if they need to get away from people, but they also need loving friends and family during difficult times to help them see the other side of the situation. A caution to well-meaning friends: some space is required—don't suffocate a Melancholy with help.

Basic Needs

Melancholies need true friends who will model God's grace and unconditional love. They need help seeing the big picture, because they often miss the forest for the trees. While you would do well *not* to try and jolly up the depressed Melancholy, they do need a little levity in the situation. Be sincere and encouraging.

Quiet, alone time is needed for Melancholies to work out their thoughts and emotions. Your best course of action is to give them space —yes, they actually need *no* people while they talk to God and mentally work through the truths of the issue. Perhaps feeling helpless, you can pray and trust God who speaks to the heart with a still, small voice. When you do have opportunity to speak, be sensitive to feelings and gently draw out as much as they will share. Find ways to quietly let them know you're in their corner and love them.

Is There Such a Thing as a Melancholy/Sanguine or Sanguine/Melancholy Combination?

Although a few personality testing devices allow for this type of combination, a Melancholy/Sanguine or Sanguine/Melancholy combo is unnatural. It causes an internal struggle between opposites. I experienced this phenomenon within myself for years before I finally gave up and accepted the "me" God created. Because I grew up thinking I was a Sanguine/Melancholy mix, I constantly felt at odds with myself, going back and forth between being spontaneous and planned, negative and positive, outgoing and shy. I often wondered who I really was inside.

Talk Easy Listen Hard

Once I learned that an individual usually has a primary and a secondary personality—and that they need to be complementary, not opposite—I reevaluated myself. I figured my Sanguine tendencies were strongest, so then I had to decide whether my Sanguine was mixed with Phlegmatic or Choleric (since Melancholy was opposite and out of the running). Seeing as I have absolutely no innate ability to relax and go with the flow (Phlegmatic), I figured I had to be Choleric. But that was a hard pill to swallow, because I didn't want to be a bossy leader (which is how I identified the Choleric personality).

Finally, I met Marita Littauer at a conference and had the opportunity to ask her about my dilemma. She put one of her books in my hand and told me to come back after I read the pages she recommended if I still had questions. Sure enough, the book answered my debate with myself by asking, of all things, if I fold my underwear or just stuff it into the drawer! While I fold my husband's and daughter's undergarments, I never take time to fold my own—after all, no one ever sees them and the wrinkles stretch out once I'm wearing them. Bingo! That response was listed almost word-for-word as the reply of a practical, no-nonsense Sanguine/Choleric.

Notable Quotables

"Only Christ can free us from the prison of legalism, and then only if we are willing to be freed."

MADELEINE L'ENGLE

Yikes! I didn't want to be Choleric! After all, my dad had often said to me, "Don't you grow up to be a bossy woman like either one of your grandmothers!" (Both my maternal and paternal grandmothers were known as strong, opinionated women.) And I thought the Bible taught that women were to be submissive to men—didn't it? Could a woman be Choleric? So I searched the Scriptures and read what the Bible says about women and submission, and I realized there are only two arenas in which God sets up a man over women—in the church and in marriage. And in both, God's purpose is protection. No, it is not wrong or unspiritual for a woman to be Choleric.

When I finally asked God to forgive me for my wrong thinking and gave myself permission to utilize my Choleric strengths, I experienced such a great sense of freedom and peace. I stopped striving to be something I wasn't and released myself to be the person God created. Of course I needed to make many adjustments over the next several weeks and months. Sometimes I went overboard, and other times I reverted back to those learned struggles between opposites. But finally I've learned to accept my natural strengths and also utilize the learned strengths of the Melancholy —traits I learned from my parents in childhood. Now I don't kick against my Choleric desires and tendencies, but I try to incorporate those strengths into my life.

Do you struggle with perceiving yourself as Sanguine/ Melancholy or Melancholy/Sanguine? Try asking yourself these questions. Do I want to do what's best (a) to please the other person, or (b) because that's the right thing to do? (a) Do I like change and can be flexible, or (b) does a sudden change in plans throw me for a loop? Sanguine people will choose a's while Melancholies choose b's.

More often than not, this particular dilemma applies to women. We can ask ourselves: Was my mother a Sanguine or Melancholy? (Some learned tendencies come from mothers.) Were you more Sanguine up until you got married and had children? (Marriage and motherhood almost always causes women to demonstrate more Melancholy-type organizational skills and attention to detail.)

The other consideration that might help you decide your primary personality is looking at which personality is *least* like you? In my situation, I have virtually no Phlegmatic strengths. Therefore, I must possess some Choleric tendencies. In the end, I decided I am probably about seventy percent Sanguine, twenty percent Choleric, and the other ten percent includes Melancholy traits learned from my parents.

Don't forget that it is reasonable—even desirable—to end up in adulthood with combinations of many positive traits from all of the personality types. However, even though I might acquire learned traits from other personality types, when I get fatigued, sick, and stressed, the things I have learned fall away, and I must be able to cope with the real me!

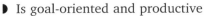

COMBO ANYONE? When combined with Choleric tendencies:

▶ Is goal-oriented and productive
▶ Gives excellent constructive criticism
▶ Can be a peaceful arbitrator

When combined with Phlegmatic tendencies:

▶ Analyzes and appraises—behind the scenes
▶ Quiet, reserved, and retiring
▶ Introverted and soft-spoken

Gotta Have It!

Needs . . .

▶ To attain a bit of perfection in various areas of life
▶ Others' sensitivity to their moods
▶ Others who take them seriously—not too much teasing
▶ A safe friend with whom to share
▶ Time away from people to recharge
▶ Time and space to think before speaking
▶ Respect—not silliness—when they are being serious
▶ Factual, orderly details when talking through a situation
▶ Gentle encouragement to look at the positive parts of situations
▶ Patient help to see the good in self and others
▶ Help to become a person of praise

THE GOD FACTOR

Melancholies are capable of knowing God on a deep and intimate level. Think of the Psalms written by David as he tended the sheep in the quiet, lonely fields of his homeland. David expressed great joy and deep sorrow. Scripture makes it obvious his sin profoundly impacted his emotions and thoughts, yet elation with his loving, merciful, forgiving God was just as evident. Perhaps more than any other personality, Melancholies know how to be quiet and listen to their inner thoughts and the still small voice of God.

But Melancholies, driven by the need for order, observe the disorderly and chaotic world around them and ask, "Why, God?"

Seeking perfection, they ask how a perfect God can allow such blatant sin and wrongdoing in His perfectly created world. They also often get bogged down in the more legalistic aspects of Christianity, which can easily become a debilitating list of do's and don'ts and can usurp a joyful relationship with the Living God.

**Key Verse
for the Melancholy**

"It is for freedom that Christ has set us free. Stand firm, then, and do not let yourselves be burdened again by a yoke of slavery."

GALATIANS 5:1

The Bible refers to us as *jars of clay*, fragile, breakable vessels filled with the treasure of the Spirit of God. We are fallible creatures with whom the Almighty God wants to relate, fill, and use—by His grace and with His power. The Melancholies would do well to read and apply the truths found in the jars of clay chapter (2 Corinthians 4) as they seek to live a perfect life in an imperfect, sinful world where nothing ultimately matters but God's love and grace.

Once Melancholies experience God's justification, grace, and forgiveness, they can possess a spiritual freedom from the fear of failure.

Released by God's work in their own lives, they become more forgiving, gracious people, intent on communicating God's grace to others. They still innately work toward perfection and seek to fulfill the Lord's commands, but they also demonstrate deep and abiding love for those around them as they become others centered. They make wonderful hands, arms, and feet in the body of Christ—serving the Church with humility, obedience, perseverance, care, and a sound mind.

Communication Clues

A few sensitive words are needed by Melancholies. Respect their time, space, and silence. Don't pry—let them tell you when they are ready, on their terms. In conversation, stick to facts and orderly, organized details—not a lot of meaningless chitchat. You need to listen to what they say and be sensitive to moods to be able to laugh and cry with them.

Don't be too happy, it makes the Melancholy want to throw up! I learned this lesson while occasionally riding along with my husband

Talk Easy Listen Hard

during the season of his life that he enjoyed a truck-driving career. On one overnight trip, I remember waking up in the sleeper compartment behind the driver's seat hearing Rich ranting and raving first about how the loading dock was situated and then the way the men were unloading his truck. Nothing suited him, and he very vocally continued complaining as the unloading continued. I quickly popped up into the passenger seat with the goal of compensating for the negative words filling the driving compartment. I tried (as a Sanguine) to balance out my Choleric/Melancholy's barrage of negativity. For every negative word he said, I had a positive comment. Suddenly in a moment of silence, my most recent words froze and seemed to hang in the air for a moment—a split second in which I heard the sappy, too-sweet words and realized how unhelpful and insincere I sounded. For the Melancholy's sake, be real, be sincere, or don't say anything at all.

General Communication Characteristics of a Melancholy:

- Thinks internally
- What is said aloud is meant
- Uses few gestures; little touch
- Very little dramatic facial expression
- Very selective with whom they share
- Communicates on a need-to-know basis
- A good listener—patient, attentive, sensitive to feelings
- Withdraws if insecure about outcome of conversation
- Dismisses compliments and does not issue them to others
- Generally shares negative observations
- Can be too detail oriented; boring

FOR WOMEN
Experiencing a Melancholy Man

As you sit at the kitchen table, surrounded by travel brochures and vacation information, you wonder how fast he'll shoot down whatever suggestions you make about the family's summer trip you're trying to plan.

Just then he walks into the room, surveys the messy array on the table, and puts his hands on his hips. "How's it going? Are you making any progress?" He's frowning at the scattered maps and fliers.

Since you did not expect him to ask for a report at this moment, you scramble to find the three top destinations you think everyone might enjoy. But as you begin showing him and explaining, he calmly shoots holes in each idea. The sad thing is, Mr. Practical is right about everything. You know you shouldn't take it personally, but you spent a lot of time working on this—okay not as much as *he* would have spent. Arrgh!

In frustration, you throw the papers you've been holding onto the table and shout, "If you know so much about everything, *you* plan the darn vacation!" Then you feel even more miserable when he looks sad, turns, and walks quietly out of the kitchen. "I didn't mean that the way it sounded," you call after him. Sitting down again, you rest your hands on the paper-piled table and implore God to erase your harsh words, give you patience, and remind you of all the things you love about your husband. You just want to plan a vacation everyone will love!

What makes my Melancholy guy tick?

Your Melancholy initially wowed you with his ability to do things perfectly and keep everything running smoothly. In fact, you probably felt honored and a bit in awe that such an amazing person would want to marry *you*! He was the epitome of order and perfection—your Mr. Perfect!

Soon he's driving you nuts! He's too perfect—and he expects perfection from you too. He inevitably sees the negative side of every situation and bursts all your creative bubbles. He nitpicks and complains about almost everything and everyone. Of course, when under attack (from you or others) he becomes quiet and sullen, and withdraws into his shell. Then he can be antisocial, looking down his perfect nose at you and every other imperfect mortal. This may be what it seems like to you on the outside looking in, but there is much more than you realize going on inside his head and heart.

Your melancholy is a deep, analytical thinker who needs you to help him balance the depth of his personality with the imperfect and uncaring world. Be there for him when he reaches out—be sensitively quiet and affirming and listen attentively when he's ready to share. Express your appreciation for the things he adds to your life and good he brings to the world—but center your praise on *who he is* more than what he does.

How do I get him to lighten up and be more positive?

Melancholies can experience joy much more often than real happiness, because their happiness is based on perfection while joy is from the Lord. The best way to help your Melancholy lighten up and enjoy the world around him is to pray for his relationship with God, using prayers from Scripture, adapted and personalized for your guy, for example: Ephesians 3:16–19; Philippians 1:9–11; Colossians 1:9–12.

Practical ways to help your guy enjoy the lighter side of life include planning—with his approval and support—fun things to do together, such as outdoor activities, going to a sporting event, or playing together at an amusement park. Remember to ask him to reserve the date on the calendar, and make sure the activity is something you both enjoy. Then go and have fun together.

E

1:17–19

"I keep asking that the God of our Lord Jesus Christ, the glorious Father, may give you the Spirit of wisdom and revelation, so that you may know him better. I pray also that the eyes of your heart may be enlightened in order that you may know the hope to which he has called you, the riches of his glorious inheritance in the saints, and his incomparably great power for us who believe."

EPHESIANS 1:17–19

FOR MEN
Experiencing the Melancholy Woman

You realize you've been staying late at work on purpose lately, because you dread going home. Your wife always seems to have a list as long as her arm of things that need to be done around the house. Isn't it enough that you bring home the bacon? You make a good salary, there is always money in the bank, so why can't she just hire a handyman to do the work?

The Analytical Melancholy

Pulling into the garage and turning off the engine of the car, you sit still for a moment reveling in the quiet. You summon your reserve strength to face a big to-do list and the little woman. As you sit there, you look around at the meticulously cared for garage walls. Every tool and piece of equipment is hung in place—thanks to your wife. As a matter of fact, you muse, you really do appreciate the well-cared-for environment your wife creates in your home. You look at the clean tools—she's even willing to clean up the mess you make when you get around to doing the odd jobs.

You finally make your way into the house and are happy to sniff dinner smells. There she is in the kitchen, everything under control. The baby is sitting in the high chair, content with the cereal she's half eating, half playing with. Yep, life is good, and you need to tell your wife how much you appreciate her role in your happiness. You walk over to the sink and kiss the back of her neck.

"Hey, I didn't even hear you come in." She turns and grabs a dish towel to dry her hands. "Did you remember to get milk at the store on the way home? I left you a message at work." She looks at your embarrassed expression and laughs, "Don't worry, I'll run out and get some after dinner if you watch the baby. I need the off-duty time anyway."

She whirls around to finish putting supper on the table, but you stop her, look into her eyes and say gently and sincerely, "Have I told you lately how much I love you and how very much I appreciate all the little things you do to keep our lives running smoothly?"

She gives a little self-conscious smile and shakes her head. "Anybody could do what I do. I'm not that special, but I appreciate you saying so." You grin—she can do almost anything but receive a compliment graciously.

What makes my Melancholy woman tick?

Many women claim to be at least a little Melancholy, probably because of all the details in most women's lives. But the proof of a true Melancholy woman is her naturally negative perspective—but wait, that's not a bad thing! Because she thinks from the negative side of any equation and eliminates the reasons a theory will *not* work, when she finally comes to a conclusion she's almost always right. She

Talk Easy Listen Hard

might not make as many decisions as the decisive Choleric or the leap-first-think-later Sanguine, but hers will be wise and solid.

Your Melancholy will probably be schedule-oriented, function well alone, and not mind doing menial, detailed work. Speaking of a schedule, Melancholies often can't function without a schedule and can become obsessed with punctuality. She may be health and nutrition conscious, but unlike the Sanguine who may try every new diet that comes along for two days or less, the Melancholy sticks to a routine.

Also note that her perfectionism may cause procrastination. If she can't get the laundry folded and perfectly put away in the drawers before dinner, it might sit around for a while until she finds time to get back to the job and perfect it. She might not take well to the idea of putting the folded piles back into the laundry basket, so instead she leaves it in the laundry room until she has time to finish the project—out of sight is out of mind and she wants to finish the job *right*.

My husband came up with a wonderful cure for my moodiness early in our marriage (even though I'm a high Sanguine, this idea seems to work for women across the board). When I displayed a grouchy mood, he would suggest I eat something or take a nap—and it worked! With the Melancholy, all she might need is permission to go into the bedroom, lie down, and have a little quiet time away from the rest of the world. Caution: do not try to joke and tease her into a better mood—she won't appreciate your efforts. Be sensitive and encouraging, giving her time, space, and silence if she wants it.

How do I get her to love me for who I am and stop criticizing me for what I do or don't do?

The big reason a Melancholy is irritable is because something in her life is out of sorts—and it isn't always you, although you can feel like you are the result or target of her frustration. If you can sensitively draw out of her a better explanation of the problem, you may be able to help fix it or help by giving her a more realistic perspective on the situation. Sometimes, though, she won't share with you and you will be hard-pressed to figure out the cause of her unhappiness.

Even if she seems to be targeting your mistakes in her complaints, you may not be the main cause of her displeasure. Try to remain objective, not taking her attacks personally. If you can do something about her complaint, do it—if not, give it, and her, over to the Lord and ask for peace and wisdom. Remember there are things inside her head you cannot see and do not know about unless she shares them.

In the overall picture, helping her develop artistic or musical talents may give her the needed release from some of the intense emotions she is experiencing. When she's upset, you might encourage her to work out her emotions by playing the piano, listening to music, picking up her paints and expressing her feelings on a canvas, going to her aerobics class, or writing a poem.

The Bible speaks of a woman who nitpicks and criticizes in Proverbs 19:13 as a quarrelsome wife who is like a constant dripping. We had a sink in our basement bathroom that dripped for several months. The annoying sound of *drip—drip—drip* was enough to make you mad. And the sink corroded where the drips constantly landed, wearing away the surface. Is she wearing you down? Take it to the Lord and then gently and sensitively speak with her about how her words and attitude are affecting you.

BOTTOM LINE

Goals for the Melancholy:

▶ Practice making positive statements and observations
▶ Celebrate incremental improvement
▶ Realize that perfectionism often causes procrastination
  —and just do it!
▶ Ease up on your standards for yourself and others
▶ Learn to appreciate differences and look less for perfection
▶ Speak up more often, and risk sharing what is in your mind and heart
▶ Express feelings and communicate needs rather than withdrawing

Talk Easy Listen Hard

Tips for the Person Relating to the Melancholy:

▶ Give sincere compliments at appropriate times
▶ Help your Melancholy see the whole picture with a realistic perspective
▶ Help your Melancholy develop healthy forms of expression
▶ Respect the Melancholy's time, personal space, and moods
▶ Don't try to meet their expectations of perfection; be yourself
▶ Give them concrete guidelines, clear expectations, and orderly details
▶ Remember they like to live by a schedule
▶ Give opportunities to talk deeply about interests and concerns

Praying **for My Melancholy**

Thank You for this careful, cautious person
who takes such good care of the details of our lives.
Help me remember to give _____ quiet time and space,
accurate details, and specific expectations. Help me to be
persistent and prayerful in sharing encouragement and joy.

TIME TOGETHER FOR THE TWO OF YOU

These questions are specifically designed for a couple in which one person or both people exhibit Melancholy qualities (if neither of you tend to be Melancholy, skip to the next chapter). If your partner is unwilling or unable to work with you, partner with God as you work through the following questions and ideas.

1. Which one of you has Melancholy tendencies and to what degree (**1**—not much at all–**10**—could be a poster child)?

2. Brainstorm a list of strengths the Melancholy brings to your relationship.

3. This question is for the non-Melancholy partner. Give an example of a recent time when your Melancholy pointed out your failure or complained about something you did or didn't do correctly—and how you felt about it. How could they have better approached the problem and been more helpful and encouraging?

4. Look back to the Bottom Line tips. Have the Melancholy partner look over the list and say which items would be especially appreciated from the other person.

5. Discuss whether your Melancholy is mostly purebred or mixed with Choleric or Phlegmatic—and how that makes them unique.

6. End your time together by having the non-Melancholy partner pray, thanking God for the specific Melancholy strengths that God fearfully and wonderfully created within that special person.

CHAPTER

tHe Retiring PHLegMatic

Phillip Phlegmatic opened one eye and then the other, watching the bedroom slowly come into focus. He knew from the amount of light in the room that he had slept well into the morning. Peggy's side of the bed was predictably cold—she'd probably been up for hours. She must have received his and her energy allotments when God parceled them out!

He stretched and gave serious thought to rolling over and going back to sleep, when Peggy breezed into the bedroom with a huge stack of neatly folded laundry. "Rise and shine. It's a great day to mow the lawn."

How could she possibly be so cheerful about the concept of mowing the lawn? Probably because she didn't have to do it. Come to think, though, she mowed it last week. Phillip grunted and slowly made his way into the bathroom.

"Hurry up, dear," Peggy said, reaching around him to get something in the cabinet under the sink, "because the bathroom is the next project on my list for this afternoon."

That pulled him up short—this afternoon? "What time is it? Did I sleep past noon?" Phillip stifled a yawn. "How can you be so chipper when you came to bed after I did last night?" he growled. "Can't we take a day off and goof off, just me and you?" He gave her his particularly persuasive smile—the one that used to work.

No luck this time. Peggy frowned and pulled out her list. He hated lists.

"Maybe some other time, bud, but we've got to get moving on the chores around here. I don't see anyone else waiting to do them." She began spraying something with fumes that made him gag.

"Okay, okay," Phillip said from the bedroom, "you win. I'm going out to mow the lawn. Just let me grab a bite of breakfast—ah, lunch."

Sound like anyone you know?

You might be Phlegmatic if:

HIM HER

☐ ☐ You are generally quiet, enjoying watching others rather than participating

☐ ☐ You can deliver a joke without cracking a smile

☐ ☐ You only say something when you truly mean it

☐ ☐ You are able to calm others in stressful situations

☐ ☐ You consider yourself to be relaxed and laid-back

☐ ☐ You would rather be with one or two friends than in a crowd of people

GOTTA KNOW INFO

If you've gotten to this point in the book and feel like you or your honey characterize a little of all of the personality types, you are probably Phlegmatic. Studies show a whooping 69 percent of any given population is Phlegmatic. This group literally holds the world together like duct tape. Cholerics (3 percent) envision plans for the future, Sanguines (11 percent) get everyone excited and motivated about the plans, and Melancholies (17 percent) run feasability studies, plan the budget, and draw up blueprints. But the Phlegmatics are the laborers who put in the gazillion hours of grunt work—and they are far less appreciated, lauded and respected as the other more up-front people. Don't underestimate the goodness and value of this quiet chameleon who keeps the peace and fills in the cracks.

Biblical Bio:

The Apostle John

John, the disciple whom Jesus loved, was most likely a strong, silent, peace-loving Phlegmatic. Always at Jesus' side, he wrote about Jesus as Friend, Shepherd, and Savior.

Good News

Phlegmatics are generally stable, agreeable, and content, remaining somewhere in the background of the total picture. More loyal than a golden retriever, Phlegmatics are easygoing, supportive, and great listeners. In fact, at first glance these people seem perfect. After reading about the weaknesses of the other three personalities, we appreciate the Phlegmatics and their low-key emotions, adaptable nature, and cooperative spirit.

Challenging News

The longer you know a Phlegmatic, the more they may test your patience. Phlegmatics hide their emotions and thoughts so well, you might feel like you don't know them well after years of friendship. You may begin to notice that they will say and do almost anything to keep the peace. Is that being tactful, compromising, or lying?

Phlegmatics are better followers than leaders, particularly when it comes to making decisions. But if they don't agree with the person in charge or the order that's been issued, they can become stubborn, sullen, and refuse to cooperate. Their greatest defensive weapon is procrastination.

Under Stress

Under fire, Phlegmatics retreat. Seldom do they stick around to explain or defend themselves. They avoid conflict and stress like the plague. When life in general gets too stressful or busy, they move slower, procrastinate, and sometimes appear lazy—when they are just plain tired.

When the volume of life's chaos and clatter get turned on high, Phlegmatics tune out. And because life in today's society moves at a fast and furious pace, Phlegmatics can experience the feelings of insecurity and worthlessness that produce the hopeless expression, "Why bother?" For some, a simple nap or hike in the woods brings refreshment and a more positive outlook, but others sink into depression. Remember that Phlegmatics don't readily share their feelings and thoughts with others, so you may not know until it's too late.

Basic Needs

Mellow and low-key, Phlegmatics are low-maintenance friends. In fact, it is easy—but unfair—to take them for granted. Just because they are not as funny and entertaining as the Sanguine, as accomplished as the Choleric, or as practical as the Melancholy, the Phlegmatic still needs appreciation and ego reinforcement.

Phlegmatics crave peace, so don't rock the boat! They'd like to live without stress, with a sense of sameness, in a world of tranquility where everyone gets along. While this is not always possible, try to provide your Phlegmatic with a little rest and quiet in every day.

Probably the number one thing Phlegmatics need from the rest of the world is reduced expectations. They just don't accomplish as much, move as fast, or speak as freely as the other three personality types—and that is okay. Give each person in your life permission to be the unique being God designed.

COMBO ANYONE?

When combined with Melancholy tendencies:

▶ Introverted—recharges on quiet time
▶ Accomplishes behind-the-scenes tasks effectively without limelight
▶ Compassionate listener and deep, internal thinker

When combined with Sanguine tendencies:

▶ Quite the comedian—dry humor
▶ Easygoing—a favorite friend
▶ Completely relationship-oriented—never seems to get anything done

Gotta Have It!
Needs . . .

▶ A peaceful environment
▶ Respect and a feeling of worth
▶ Quiet, understated praise, recognition, and attention
▶ Patient, focused attention
▶ Lots of sleep and down time
▶ Realistic expectations from others
▶ Assistance and assurance when making decisions
▶ Help with self-discipline and setting up routines
▶ A quiet, peaceful place to live
▶ A home that feels safe from the pressures of the world
▶ Encouragement—verbal and practical

THE GOD FACTOR

Like Melancholies, Phlegmatics are quiet, internal thinkers. Mary, the mother of Jesus, might have been Phlegmatic—we know she observed everything going on with her little boy and "treasured all these things in her heart" (Luke 2:51).

Phlegmatics naturally possess many godly qualities such as peace, compassion, gentleness, tenderness, and patience. But do not mistake the peaceful Phlegmatic for a spiritual giant. While they tend to understand relationships and can tune in to God, just like everybody else each Phlegmatic is born a sinner needing to confess Jesus as Lord and Savior before beginning a personal relationship with God.

When Phlegmatics grasp the concept of regeneration (having been made brand-new, complete in Christ), they become Christ centered, joyful, and courageous. As they grow in maturity and know God more, their confidence in Him and in what He can do in and through them grows.

Because the Christian life is full of spiritual disciplines, Phlegmatics need to apply Hebrews 12:11 to their lives: "No discipline seems pleasant at the time, but painful. Later on, however, it produces a harvest of righteousness and *peace* for those who have been trained by it." (emphasis added).

Key Verse
for the Phlegmatic

"Peace I leave with you; my peace I give you. I do not give to you as the world gives. Do not let your hearts be troubled and do not be afraid."

John 14:27

In 1 Timothy 6:6, Paul writes, "godliness with contentment is great gain." Unlike the peaceful, content Phlegmatic, the Choleric apostle Paul admitted in Philippians 4:12 that he had to *learn* the secret of contentment. Indeed, the Phlegmatic is so relaxed that others can often simmer down in their presence and find rest. This makes the Phlegmatic an excellent counselor, shepherding or visitation pastor, or comforter in the medical profession. Filled with the Spirit of God, this person has boldness to serve and touch lives that need the healing, soothing peace of God.

Where the Melancholy fears failure, Phlegmatics fear the unknown. Here again it is Paul who addresses the problem in 2 Timothy 1:7 with these words, "God did not give us a spirit of timidity, but a spirit of power, of love and of self-discipline." Strong and wise words to help the Phlegmatic be all they can be for God's Kingdom work.

COMMUNICATION CLUES

Show your Phlegmatic your respect and admiration. Give praise and attention whenever possible. Because Phlegmatics don't

Talk Easy Listen Hard

call attention to themselves or accomplish great things on a daily basis, it may be hard to come up with a long list of accolades—but you need to make an effort to show your appreciation for the person inside.

Realize that Phlegmatics are internal thinkers. They don't talk all the time, so pay attention when they do and recognize that what they say is usually worth hearing. Discipline yourself to give focused, patient attention, and wait until they are finished talking before you respond.

Sometimes just being in the same room or going out together —even when neither of you is talking—can communicate your respect for the person and desire to be with them. Don't push Phlegmatics to speak or give an answer within your time frame— be patient. Try to restrain from overloading Phlegmatics with too many details or responsibilities. Show that you're in this together!

Where the Sanguine is a people-pleaser and flits from flower to flower, the Phlegmatic is usually deeply loyal to just a handful of friends. If you are Sanguine, remember to stop and smell the roses with your Phlegmatic honey. They will enjoy hearing about you and your day, but will also want to talk about themselves sometimes. Be sensitive and affirming.

General Communication Characteristics of a Phlegmatic:

- Uses relaxed body language
- Uses soft voice
- Uses dry humor
- Calms others during stressful times
- Speaks few words, seldom—but meaningfully
- Doesn't want to get involved
- Waits to share until internal thoughts are completely formulated
- Often misses opportunities to share because they are busy processing
- Often misses opportunities because of a fear of the unknown
- Seldom voices opinions (only to safe people)

FOR WOMEN
Experiencing a Phlegmatic Man

What happened to this house? "Jere, where are you?" You walk further into the chaotic mess, putting your packages on the dining room table—the only clear spot you see. Toys literally cover the floor, except for some crackers and spilled cereal. You step around a turned-over chair. You only left him with the kids for two hours! For goodness sake, he manages the whole accounting department at his company. How could this have happened?

Following the trail of devastation, you arrive at the den where two-year-old Katie is sitting on Jere's prone form leaning against the couch with the baby propped in one arm. His other hand is loosely holding a stuffed teddy bear. Cartoons are blaring, but Katie's high-pitched squealing almost drowns them out when she sees you.

You silence the television and turn just in time to grab her before she rubs the chocolate on her face into your favorite pair of slacks. "Run to the bathroom and climb into the tub, little lady, where we can get you cleaned up!" She scampers off.

"How did you do that?" Jere has opened one eye and is looking at you with awe.

"What do you mean?" What is he talking about? Looking around the room, you don't know whether to laugh or cry. Why in the world did you think a couple hours out shopping with some girl-friends would be a treat? This trio has made more work for you in two hours than a whole day of regular keep-up-with-them chores.

"She went."

"Jere, you're not making sense. Who went? Where?"

Jere struggled into a more upright position and woke the baby in the process. He looks exhausted. "Katie wouldn't do anything I asked her to do all night."

"*All night* was only two hours." You take Emily from him, realizing immediately why she's uncomfortable. "When is the last time you changed her?"

"Changed her?" He has the decency to look embarrassed. "Maybe that's why she was fussy. I'm sure glad you're home!" He's finally standing beside you. "Sorry the place is a little messed up."

Talk Easy Listen Hard

He swallows hard. "I don't know how you do it. Look, I'll go help Katie with her bath."

"Thanks. I'll change the baby and then start on clean-up patrol. What did you *do* for the past two hours?"

"Whatever Katie thought was fun." His expression makes you chuckle. "Raising kids is hard work. I don't think I'll mind going to work tomorrow morning."

An hour later, the house is back to normal, the kids are asleep, and you walk into the master bedroom hoping Jere will hold to the commitment he made yesterday in church. You were so excited when he responded to the Sunday School teacher's call for each husband to commit to lead his wife and family in daily devotions. Jere had suggested on the way home that the two of you start reading the Bible and praying before bed each night. Last night, Emily was sick and needed you for a long time, so you'd told Jere the two of you would have to start tonight. From the snoring lump in the bed, you regretfully acknowledge that tonight's a wash too.

Lord, Jere's a great guy and a good dad, but could you please help him be a spiritual leader in this home? Give him strength and desire, Lord. And help me be patient in the meantime.

What makes my Phlegmatic *guy* tick?

He's the strong, silent type—with the emphasis on silent. When you first met him, there was ample opportunity to imagine that he was thinking romantic thoughts about you. As a relationship-oriented guy, he scored big points when he listened to you for hours on end. Because he hates conflict, he never disagreed with you—and you thought he was agreeing with every word you said. In moments of trauma, he was calm, patient, and relaxed—breaking any tension with his dry humor or soft, sensible response. He calmed you down, soothed all your stresses, and never argued—what more could you ask?

But as the months and years go by, he begins to drive you crazy because he will not give you a straight answer. You ask what he likes—he doesn't care. You want to know how he wants you to do something—he doesn't care. Doesn't he care about *you* anymore? He's so hard to talk to—it takes him forever to respond!

Besides that, he's so lazy and undisciplined—low energy, sleeps a lot, and procrastinates all the time! You can no longer remember what you initially thought was so exciting about Mr. Dull. He agrees with *everybody*, compromises his standards, and lets others make all the decisions. You can't get a single opinion out of him. In fact, the harder you press him to express his opinions, the more stubbornly silent he becomes.

How do I encourage him to be the real leader of our home?

The number one problem expressed to me by Christian women today is a lack of godly leadership in Christian homes. Let me suggest that the answer to our woes lies in part within this section of this chapter. If over two-thirds of the Christian men in marriages today are Phlegmatic, leadership is indeed a concern for Christian women. Let me explain, though, why it is our problem and not theirs!

Generally a Phlegmatic person goes unnoticed, because he doesn't do anything with great pizzazz. However, some of his strengths include loyalty, consistency, and perseverance. About the only place Phlegmatic man is noticed is at work—and that's after several years of doing the same thing day in and day out—and for this he receives a promotion. After several promotions, he finds himself in management, with a leader-type role that he did not ask for, but won't cause waves over by rejecting. Actually, when he finally learns the new job, he turns into a fine manager because of his natural rapport with people—and so he gets promoted again.

By now, you are totally bewildered: he is getting rave reviews at the office, but at home he is more unmotivated than ever. He's mostly useless around the house and leaves even major decisions to you.

Stop for a moment and think about his internal wiring. His natural Phlegmatic disposition recoils from conflict, but he must mediate several times every day at work. He no longer does mindless, repetitive duties, but must think on his feet and communicate nearly the whole day. By the time he gets home, all his learned

Talk Easy Listen Hard

skills and abilities have been taxed to the limit. Maybe he needs a less stressful, more low-key job, but he relishes the respect he gets at work and knows the family depends on his income. He's stuck between a rock and a hard place—and he needs an understanding wife at home to help him salvage a little rest, peace, and tranquility from the time he spends at home. Don't forget that he needs your affirmation, admiration, and approval in the small things that often get overlooked.

So what does this have to do with leadership? The Phlegmatic can be an excellent leader, but he will lead with a very different style than the outgoing, high-energy, follow-me visionary style of the Choleric—the one we think of when we say *leader*. Perhaps we women need to readjust our expectations for the man in our lives. God divided His perfect leadership skills into all four of the personality types. The Choleric leads with vision, certainty, and boldness. The Sanguine leads with pizzazz, inspiration, and enthusiasm. The Melancholy leads with precision, careful instruction, and disciplined marching orders.

Notable Quotables

"True contentment is a real, even an active virtue—not only affirmative but creative. It is the power of getting out of any situation all there is in it."

G. K. CHESTERTON

The Phlegmatic is a unique leader. He leads gently, lovingly, with a relaxed pace—and walks right alongside you. But because he's not driven to accomplish or achieve, he does only what is necessary. If he is not aware of your spiritual need for leadership, or if his idea of spiritual leadership and yours don't look the same, it may not happen. With sensitivity and a desire to truly communicate on this issue, sit down together and work out what you *both* need and want out of your spiritual relationship—then think and pray about ways to work out those needs. Remember, he's not necessarily wrong, just different!

FOR MEN
Experiencing the Phlegmatic Woman

"Honey, can you *please* keep the kids out of the dining room? I've got to make a really important overseas call." You pointedly close both doors and survey your makeshift, temporary office. This isn't working at all. Maybe you should have rented a temporary office away from home while your building downtown is being renovated. You sit down to get your notes in order and look up the phone number.

"Daddy—" A little curly head with a smear of chocolate on the chin peeks around the slowly opening door to the kitchen.

Just then your wife looks in with a worried half smile and then both heads disappear behind the closing door. That just cannot happen when you're on the phone to your new contact in Japan! You delay the call still further as you ponder the situation. Your wife is just so relaxed and laid-back that trying to be professional in this home environment is ludicrous. The kids barge in any time they please with sticky fingers that leave spots on your reports.

And now that you're home on a regular basis, you can't figure out what your wife does all day. When you get outside your so-called office the house rarely looks any better than it did earlier in the day. There are always toys lying everywhere, dishes in the sink, piles of laundry lying around the bedrooms.

"Daddy—" The same curly-headed boy and his little sister burst into the room.

You stand up, gather the kids into your arms before they can get to the table full of papers and carry them out to find their Mama. She is sitting at the kitchen table surrounded by what looks like a grocery list, today's newspaper, and a pile of coupons. "Honey, I *really* need you to take the kids and get out of the house for about an hour so I can make this important phone call." You survey her robe and slippers and hope it won't take more than ten minutes to get the house to yourself. "I'll watch the kids for five minutes while you pull on some clothes and grab your keys. Please? This is *really* important."

About twenty minutes later the house is finally silent and you pick up the phone.

What makes my Phlegmatic woman tick?

If you married an opposite, your Choleric go-get-'em style is indeed a far cry from your Phlegmatic's sweet, easygoing, steady persona. She will not be as enthusiastic, driven, or energized as you. But she *will* complement your task-oriented drive for success with her people skills, sensitivity, and intuition.

Realize that your wife does not want the amount of activity that you have, nor is she naturally able to keep up with the pace you set. Keep in mind she likes a set routine, normal expectations, and minimum change, and hates big surprises and public attention —good or bad.

How do I energize her to keep up with chores and be a more exciting companion?

Some oranges have a lot of juice and others have much less— but no matter how hard you squeeze an orange you can only get out as much juice as that orange contains. Likewise you only get out of another person what's been wired into them. You get lots of energy and pizzazz from a Sanguine/Choleric and much less enthusiasm from the Phlegmatic/Melancholy. So what do you do to adjust your own expectations and learn to appreciate what you've got?

Realize that each of the personalities is motivated differently than the others. What energizes you might not work effectively for her. For the Phlegmatic, try coming alongside with help and encouragement. Ask her to sit down with you and discuss how much she is able to do and what she enjoys doing around the house. Divide the load appropriately between the two of you—you may actually wind up with more things to do because you have the higher energy level. If there is a task neither of you enjoys doing, split it up or try doing it together.

Look at your Phlegmatic spouse realistically. By reducing your expectations and realizing she is not purposefully trying to annoy you by shirking chores, you will feel much better and become a happier person—which in turn will motivate her to keep up with the things that bring peace and contentment to you and thus to her.

Bottom Line
Goals for the Phlegmatic:

▸ Communicate your feelings so people can understand you
▸ Focus on your strengths instead of your weaknesses
▸ Enlist an accountability or prayer partner to help you stay on task
▸ Finish three projects you've been putting off and set dates to finish others
▸ Speak up and enter the conversation
▸ Think through a presentation in advance to build confidence
▸ Be positive—show enthusiasm with some body language
▸ Don't let resentment build; watch sarcasm
▸ Don't be a wet blanket on others' ideas—listen and be positive

Tips for the Person Relating to the Phlegmatic:

▸ Come alongside the Phlegmatic and show your support
▸ Recognize even small efforts with simple praise and encouragement
▸ Sincerely compliment them to other people (but don't embarrass)
▸ Provide a quiet, peaceful, safe environment at home
▸ Don't embarrass or call attention to them in public
▸ Be patient and wait for their answer
▸ Spend time together in activities that promote discussion
▸ Give aid, wisdom, and support when they must make a decision

Praying for My Phlegmatic

Thank You for my quiet, gentle sweetheart.
Help me remember to appreciate the little things that make
_____ so peaceable, loving, and content.
Help me to come alongside with energy for the tasks that
overwhelm and quietly applaud accomplishments.

Talk Easy Listen Hard

TIME TOGETHER FOR THE TWO OF YOU

These questions are specifically designed for a couple in which one person or both people exhibit Phlegmatic qualities (if neither of you tend to be Phlegmatic, skip to the next chapter). If your partner is unwilling or unable to work with you, partner with God as you work through the following questions and ideas.

1. Which one of you has Phlegmatic tendencies and to what degree (**1**—not much at all–**10**—could be a poster child)?

2. Brainstorm a list of strengths the Phlegmatic brings to your relationship.

3. Allow the non-Phlegmatic person to answer this question. What three simple things (in priority order—so they can work on one at a time) can your Phlegmatic change or do on a regular basis that will improve your relationship?

4. Look back to the Bottom Line tips. Have the Phlegmatic partner look over the list and say which items would be especially appreciated from the other person.

5. Discuss whether your Phlegmatic is mostly purebred or mixed with Melancholy or Sanguine—and how that makes them unique.

6. End your time together by having the non-Phlegmatic partner pray, thanking God for the specific Phlegmatic strengths that God fearfully and wonderfully created within that special person.

PART TWO

Thought Continuums--
Where Our Words Come From

Do you remember the first time you realized the two of you weren't on the same page? Of course, at other times, you find yourselves completing each other's sentences. This happens because our minds process information in different, yet similar ways.

As you read the following chapters describing the four thought continuums, see where you and your partner fit. Why? Because if you understand how each other thinks you'll better know the *why* behind words and actions.

Unlike having primary and secondary personality types, in the next four categories you may find you tend to favor one side or the other—or more possibly, fall somewhere between the two extremes. By the time we reach adulthood, we are *able* to take in, process, organize, and assimilate information according to all of the categories in this section of the book. But for the purpose of understanding your original core motivations, think of your *natural preferences* and *initial tendencies*. For example, I'm not an analytical thinker who hones in on details, but once I grasp the big picture and catch on to the concept, I love to add all the little icing-on-the-cake details that make something extra pleasant and special. So remember as you read to focus on your gut-level responses or first impressions and ask your partner to reveal where he or she is coming from.

> . . . focus on your gut-level responses or first impressions

The first thought continuum addresses the way we process information—*internally or externally*. The second continuum stretches between *analytical and concrete*, showing the way we prefer to take in information. The third thought continuum stresses organization of our thoughts—is a person a *systematic or random* thinker? The fourth and final pair of opposites deals with how we approach and interact with information: *analytically or globally*.

Don't forget: As you go through each chapter of this section, turn to the back of the book and chart your tendencies in appendix A. Most of all, remember this. "The Lord knows the thoughts of man" (Psalm 94:11). Ask Him to guide your thinking as you read and process the following four chapters on thought continuums.

CHAPTER

Internal vs. External

Cleaning up after our evening meal, I suddenly remember I need to talk to Rich about something. Now that I've remembered the issue, the wheels in my brain furiously race to keep up with my flight to the living room where he sits behind his newspaper. I push down the paper (first mistake) and rush into my delivery. "We always alternate visiting your family and my family at Thanksgiving and Christmas, but this year . . . " I barrel on without pausing for breath, somewhat conscious of the fact I'm interrupting his relaxation, but determined to resolve the issue at hand.

I conclude with, "So, what do you think?"

I wait.

I wait some more.

Then I decide he must not have understood something about my presentation or question. So I begin again—this time a bit faster and at a higher pitch.

At the end of this oration, I repeat the original question, "So, what do you think?"

Silence.

I wait.

He looks a bit annoyed—or maybe he's just thinking now.

I wait.

I get tired of waiting. And I begin to wonder if he is pointedly refusing to answer me.

Yet a third time I articulate my thoughts on the subject of family and holidays, and I ask, "SO, what do YOU think?"

In a defining moment, Rich responds, "Will you please shut up and LET me think!"

Are You an Internal or External Thinker?

▶ **Surrounded by a group of people, I can make small talk forever.**

NOT AT ALL TRUE OF ME.................VERY TRUE OF ME

1 — 2 — 3 — 4 — 5 — 6 — 7 — 8 — 9 — 10

▶ **If asked a question, I give an immediate answer even if I've never before pondered the issue.**

NOT AT ALL TRUE OF ME.................VERY TRUE OF ME

1 — 2 — 3 — 4 — 5 — 6 — 7 — 8 — 9 — 10

▶ **I readily share my opinion, even if no one asks for it.**

NOT AT ALL TRUE OF ME.................VERY TRUE OF ME

1 — 2 — 3 — 4 — 5 — 6 — 7 — 8 — 9 — 10

▶ **Friends regularly ask me to emcee parties and events because I facilitate well.**

NOT AT ALL TRUE OF ME.................VERY TRUE OF ME

1 — 2 — 3 — 4 — 5 — 6 — 7 — 8 — 9 — 10

- **I'm considered a talker, and I don't mind because talking helps me process a situation.**

  NOT AT ALL TRUE OF ME...............VERY TRUE OF ME

  1 — 2 — 3 — 4 — 5 — 6 — 7 — 8 — 9 — 10

- **I feel like I'm going to burst if I can't ask questions.**

  NOT AT ALL TRUE OF ME...............VERY TRUE OF ME

  1 — 2 — 3 — 4 — 5 — 6 — 7 — 8 — 9 — 10

Internal thinkers will have the lower numbers, while external thinkers will have the higher numbers. If you scored a 10 or below, you have very strong tendencies to think internally. If you scored between 45 and 50, you definitely enjoy processing your thoughts externally. How did your partner score?

GOTTA KNOW INFO

The conversation at the beginning of this chapter served as a major wake up call for me. That day in our living room, I finally got the message: Rich and I think differently! My husband needs time and quiet space to develop and analyze his thoughts. But I need to verbalize my thinking process—and I can reach a decision or sort out my thoughts all the more effectively with an interactive audience. Wow, are we different!

The changes that accompanied that realization have helped me time and time again. I have learned to seek out friends who enjoy thinking out loud with me. Then, when I really need to get through to Rich, I've already processed my thoughts and can give him the quiet space he wants to think. If I have plenty of time to make a decision on something, I might toss my options in Rich's direction and ask him to get back to me with any ideas he comes up with. On the rare occasion a situation needs an immediate response, I've learned to trust his judgment and encourage him to make the decision.

Sometimes I still irritate Rich with too much information too fast—or too many nonpertinent details. I get so overly excited about my ideas, they tumble over one another and just pour out of my mouth. These slipups tend to shut him down. He wonders if I really value what he has to say when I keep interrupting him. His contributions to the conversation often set off an exciting chain reaction of new ideas that I want to share with him immediately—before I forget them.

A review of the personality information on the Sanguine and Melancholy personality types may help you see the internal/external thinking rationale more clearly. If your primary or secondary personality is Sanguine, then you were born to talk, you love spontaneity, and most likely your creativity helps you think outside the box. Your optimistic nature helps you see all of the fabulous potentials of an idea long before you stop to consider if any of them will actually work. In fact, one possibility will ignite a second idea, which will spawn a third . . . and then you're off.

If you consider yourself to be in part Melancholy, you could loathe conversing with the person I just described. If only they would just slow down and think rationally, taking one idea at a time through a series of mental tests and analyses. That's how *your* mind works. You don't bother people with useless information—you only speak accurate truth! You might be considered by others to be a bit quiet, but what you have to say is worth listening to.

Which person in the above two paragraphs is *right*? Trick question—neither is right or wrong, just different. The key is understanding each other, learning to get along, and figuring out how to maximize situations by using these two different thinking styles to the best advantage.

Good News

Rich, my husband the internal thinker, painstakingly works through every detail and possibility—from the negative perspective. He evaluates each possible scenario by completing this statement: "This won't work, because . . ." By the time he's eliminated all of the probable reasons a situation *won't* work, he's validated that it *will* be successful. Therefore (I hate to admit it), he's almost always right.

3

On the other hand, thinking out loud does have its place . . . like when focus groups get together. A few years ago I was part of one such panel for a local amusement park. The group consisted of the person in charge, a scribe who wrote our ideas on large chart paper, and about ten of us from the community and area businesses. The leader brought up questions and allowed the ten of us to talk about our immediate reactions, opinions, and ideas—all of which were written down. Before we left, the lists of ideas were taped around the room, and we were asked to go around and choose the five best thoughts given throughout the day. Several months after the meeting, I enjoyed revisiting the park and seeing the changes and additions our group had suggested. I was gratified to know I'd been a part of the process. A focus group needs active, out-loud thinkers who bounce ideas off each other to birth new and better ideas.

Challenging News

While neither extreme is to be valued above the other, both the internal and external thinkers have legitimate gripes with one another. To the internal thinker, who rules their mouth responsibly, external thinkers appear to say things they don't mean and make commitments they don't honor. The external thinker, freely tossing ideas around, interprets the silence of internal thinkers as criticism or apathy.

Traits of the Internal Thinker:

▸ Thinks without speaking
▸ Is frustrated by interruptions when thinking
▸ Waits to share until there has been enough time to process and prepare
▸ Is quiet, reflective, and often silent
▸ Listens more than talks
▸ Has good powers of concentration
▸ May prefer to focus on one thing at a time
▸ Can feel rushed and disrespected

8

Traits of the External Thinker:

> Thinks out loud
> Becomes frustrated when the internal thinker doesn't respond promptly
> Benefits greatly from brainstorming ideas with other external thinkers
> Often talks about seedling ideas that never grow into actual events
> Talks more than listens
> Can sometimes be easily distracted
> Finds multitasking very stimulating
> Talks more when excited or nervous

THE GOD FACTOR

Why did God create these frustrating differences that make some of us want to scream and send others running for cover? We need each other. Solomon, wisest of all men, said, "There is a time for everything, and a season for every activity under heaven . . . a time to be silent and a time to speak" (Ecclesiastes 3:1, 7). The external thinker works great under pressure, with people, and without inhibitions. The internal thinker processes information carefully and methodically, makes fewer mistakes, and runs effective checks and balances. The two types of thinkers possess different abilities, which work together as two parts of the necessary whole.

Like the human body, the body of Christ has many parts. "If the whole body were an eye, where would the sense of hearing be? If the whole body were an ear, where would the sense of smell be? But in fact, God has arranged the parts in the body, every one of them, just as he wanted them to be" (1 Corinthians 12:17–18). There is no mistaking God's plan to create people different from one another—different, not better or worse. And those differences are designed to work together so that we cannot exist on our own, we need each other. And in our quest to get along, we develop more love and dependence on God and each other.

COMMUNICATING TOGETHER
Communicating with the Internal Thinker

- Give space and time to think through a situation on the person's own terms
- Don't interrupt when something is being shared
- Listen attentively (because what is being said is probably *not* just a simple idea)
- If you want to brainstorm, try someone else

Consider man's best friend, the dog. Most dog owners will tell you their dog has ways of communicating with them. While I admit that many dogs seem to have personalities and show intelligence with tricks and participation in games, bottom line: they do not talk. Therefore, even if you *think* you know what your dog is saying, you are unable to crawl into his head and make certain.

> ### Praying **for My Internal Thinker**
>
> *Thank You* for this quiet thinker. *Help me remember* to give _____ quiet space in which to process thoughts, and help me to listen attentively so that I remember what is finally said.

Likewise, even though you may think you know what is going on in the mind of the internal thinker, don't jump to conclusions. Don't pry—be patient and receptive. Remember that patience is a fruit of the Spirit (Galatians 5:22), which means only the Holy Spirit can plant it and nurture it in your life. Your job in a situation such as this is to humble yourself and ask God to grant you the self-control to keep your mouth closed, the patience to wait for the other person to respond, and the sound mind to understand and work with whatever the other person brings to the table.

When your sweetheart is ready to share, be there, be aware, and don't miss what is said! Actively attend to the conversation and respect their ideas. These disciplines and your godly attitude pay great dividends.

Communicating with the External Thinker

▶ Don't take everything said as a final answer
▶ *Before* you get too frustrated, ask to hear more another time
▶ Ask for time and space to process if you need it
▶ Give verbal encouragement and feedback

Praying for My External Thinker

Thank You for the transparency of my sweetheart.
Help me remember to appreciate the fact that I know
what is going on inside _____'s mind.
Also, give me patience to listen, wisdom to know
the truth of what is being said, and courage to speak
the truth in love when I cannot bear to listen any longer.

Because the external thinker is so closely related to the Sanguine personality style, you would do well to go back to chapter one and look at the tips on communicating with a Sanguine. Be patient when an explanation or description gets lengthy, and affirm and applaud whatever possible. Most important, if you are on the verge of overload, ask the person to share more with you at a later time.

TIME TOGETHER FOR THE TWO OF YOU

1. Compare your answers to the beginning quiz and discuss how you feel about the results.

2. Brainstorm a list of strengths the Internal Thinker brings to your relationship, and then have that person share what makes communication difficult and what would make it easier.*

3. Brainstorm a list of strengths the External Thinker brings to your relationship, and then have that person share what makes communication difficult and what would make it easier.*

4. End your time together by having both of you pray— each thanking God for specific strengths found in this chapter that make your partner a good match for you.

*If one or both of you seem balanced between these extremes, you may want to skip question 2 and/or 3.

CHAPTER

Abstract vs. Concrete

"**H**oney, what should we get your parents for Christmas?" Beth asked Tim as she put on her coat and grabbed her Bible.

"What did we get them last year?" Tim pulled the front door closed behind them and locked it. "Oh, I remember. We gave them tickets to that fancy music program." He held Beth's car door for her and then walked around and got in the driver's seat. "They seemed to enjoy that. How about sticking with a good thing?"

"I'd like to do something really special, really meaningful for them." Beth sighed and looked out the window. "They're so sweet. And they aren't getting any younger—we don't know how many more Christmases we'll have with them."

"That's a morbid thought. We just need to get them a nice gift and go on to the next person on the list."

Beth looked shocked. "Hey, that's cold. Think about how much they do for us and how dear they are. I'm so thankful they had you—for me." She elbowed him with a grin.

Tim frowned. "Beth, I love them and all, but we're talking about a simple Christmas gift here."

"Christmas gifts need to be personal. Remember, it's the thought that counts."

"Yeah, but you can think too much and waste the gray matter in your pretty little head." Tim pulled into the church lot and parked the car. Turning to Beth, he teasingly tugged on a few pieces of Beth's long blonde hair and grinned at her.

Beth looked worried. "I just want Christmas to be so special for everyone. I'll think about some ideas and get back to you for a final decision. How's that?"

"Good call since we need to get going or we'll miss the service," he teased as he opened his door to get out, throwing over his shoulder, "And with you, every day is special."

As he opened Beth's door, she grinned. "Big points, mister. Big points for that one!"

Are you an Abstract or Concrete Thinker?

▶ **People say I live with my head in the clouds.**

NOT AT ALL TRUE OF ME.................VERY TRUE OF ME
1 — 2 — 3 — 4 — 5 — 6 — 7 — 8 — 9 — 10

▶ **I like to read books like *Pilgrim's Progress* and the Narnia series.**

NOT AT ALL TRUE OF ME.................VERY TRUE OF ME
1 — 2 — 3 — 4 — 5 — 6 — 7 — 8 — 9 — 10

▶ **In an art store or museum, I gravitate toward the abstract art where I can use my imagination.**

NOT AT ALL TRUE OF ME.................VERY TRUE OF ME
1 — 2 — 3 — 4 — 5 — 6 — 7 — 8 — 9 — 10

▶ **I like to take my time making decisions and think about all the possibilities.**

NOT AT ALL TRUE OF ME.................VERY TRUE OF ME

1 — 2 — 3 — 4 — 5 — 6 — 7 — 8 — 9 — 10

▶ **On a day with big, white, puffy clouds in a blue sky, I can't help but see shapes.**

NOT AT ALL TRUE OF ME.................VERY TRUE OF ME

1 — 2 — 3 — 4 — 5 — 6 — 7 — 8 — 9 — 10

▶ **I like to imagine what heaven will be like.**

NOT AT ALL TRUE OF ME.................VERY TRUE OF ME

1 — 2 — 3 — 4 — 5 — 6 — 7 — 8 — 9 — 10

Concrete Thinkers will have the lower numbers, while Abstract Thinkers will have the higher numbers. If you scored a 10 or below, you are a very Concrete Thinker, but if you scored between 45 and 50 you definitely tend to be an Abstract Thinker. How did your partner score?

GOTTA KNOW INFO

The concrete thinker lives in the here and now, sees things in black-and-white, and sticks to facts. The abstract thinker, on the other hand, mulls things over and enjoys studying what lies beneath the surface. How frustrated one type of thinker can become with the other if they expect the other person to be the same! Just the act of acknowledging the differences in processes means you're on the right path.

In relation to personality, generally Sanguines and Cholerics are concrete thinkers. They are high energy and quite decisive, basing decisions on fact more than opinion or feelings (especially the Choleric). The abstract thinkers are the more introverted Melancholies and Phlegmatics. They like to process information slower, more quietly, and analyze everything thoroughly.

It bears repeating: the way you process thoughts is not good or bad, but something to understand and use to your advantage in each

Abstract vs. Concrete

life situation. And then, of course, after you understand your own thinking patterns, you will benefit greatly by identifying tendencies in your sweetheart in order to wisely and lovingly work together.

Good News

Abstract thinkers make wonderful inventors, composers, and poets. They are usually the dreamers, philosophers, and creatives of the world. Without them the world would be black-and-white, for they paint our world full of richly colored feelings and experiences. Even a concrete thinker, given enough time and the correct stimulus, enjoys a good story with a hidden lesson. But for the abstract thinker, time for deep thinking is a prerequisite for mental health.

Extremely concrete thinkers generally prefer to skim the newspaper over reading a science-fiction novel. These active, decisive movers-and-shakers live in the present and focus on the crisis of the moment. With sensors on high alert, their five senses gather the data they need to respond to the world around them. They smell, taste, touch, see, and hear more acutely than the abstract thinker. They don't look for hidden meanings, they just take things at face value.

Challenging News

It doesn't take a rocket scientist to picture the disaster that will occur if these two people don't understand that their differences are valuable and that they can learn to work together. The concrete thinker naturally believes the abstract thinker always has their head in the clouds and is of little practical value to the world. On the other hand, the abstract thinker can see the concrete thinker as shallow and pushy.

Traits of the Abstract Thinker:

- Imaginative and intuitive
- Dreams about possibilities
- Does not come to quick conclusions
- Enjoys stories, allegories, and analogies
- Looks for the deeper meaning, reads between the lines

Talk Easy Listen Hard

Traits of the Concrete Thinker:

▶ Likes facts and details
▶ Lives in the present, focuses on the situation at hand
▶ Can be decisive, given the facts
▶ Enjoys reading the newspaper, reports, and nonfiction
▶ Takes people and situations at face value

THE GOD FACTOR

Let's take a look back into biblical history and see examples of these two thinkers. Just like His servants in the past, God purposefully created you and your partner as two unique people for unique purposes and to work together for the good works He's planned for you (Ephesians 2:10).

The psalmist David is an excellent example of an abstract thinker. His psalms and songs to the Lord share his deep thoughts. He spent many hours, days, even years as a shepherd in his father's fields. Don't you wonder what shapes *he* saw in the clouds!

Don't you think Paul was probably a concrete thinker? He was incredibly intelligent and spent time at Mars Hill talking with the philosophers of the day, but more often he made quick decisions, demonstrated practical skills, and kept up a grueling schedule as he traveled (except when he got stuck in jail—and then he used the time to write letters).

Please don't be discouraged if you see yourself in one category and wish you were something different. Don't forget that the wise Creator perfectly designed you (with holes) to be the person He will enable you to become. *And* He has a plan to use you and your partner together for Kingdom work—so keep looking to Him to teach you who you are, how He's designed your partner, and how He wants to bring the two of you together to bless your world.

COMMUNICATING TOGETHER
Communicating with the Abstract Thinker

▶ Be patient, knowing you can benefit from their in-depth understanding

- Allow time for processing and response
- List the facts so the person has something tangible to focus on during discussion
- Appreciate their creative mind
- If you need a decision quickly, defer to the concrete thinker

Praying **for My Abstract Thinker**

Thank You for this inventive, imaginative partner. *Help me remember* to appreciate _____'s depth and creativity, and to be patient in discussions. Help me learn how to gently steer the conversation back to the facts and decisions at hand when needed.

Be patient with the abstract thinker. Every once in a while, you may feel like you're reeling them back in from "la-la land." This still does not make you right and the other person wrong. You've heard the expression, "Good things take time." In a situation where deep insight and understanding are needed, the abstract thinker is invaluable. However, if the situation calls for an immediate decision based on facts, remind them of your differences and suggest an appropriate decision based on the facts at hand. Try to value the other person during this interchange so you don't come across as arrogant. At other times when you need their ability to be creative and think below the surface, take advantage of their mental prowess and give them deserved praise.

Communicating with the Concrete Thinker

- Communicate factually and briefly when short on time or in a tense moment
- Ask *why* and *how* to get them to think more deeply with you
- Explain how your topic is relevant and affects them
- Only bring emotions into the discussion if there is adequate time
- Appreciate this person's ability to make quick decisions

Talk Easy Listen Hard

Praying for My Concrete Thinker

Thank You for this black-and-white, see-it-as-it-is person who can be so practical. *Help me remember* to focus more on the here and now when talking to _____, yet gently add depth to our conversations when there is enough time to relax.

Sometimes it can feel like your concrete thinker lives entirely on life's surface. You just can't get the person to think deeply. They are always so busy and preoccupied with the here and now, there's no time to sit and talk with you about things that really matter. Don't give up. Try expressing your need to talk deeply and ask to set aside time once in a while to think together. You could suggest reading a book and discussing it, or choose a topic or question to examine together. The problem is not that concrete thinkers cannot think deeply, they just get so wrapped up in immediate concerns that they usually don't take the time unless they see the need.

Do you sometimes feel like this person is not close to God because they don't spend the time praying and reading the Word like you do? Pray about your concern, but realize that a devotional time with God might not necessarily mean the same thing to the two of you. Concrete thinkers register information directly through the senses, so a walk in the great outdoors or even a beautifully scented candle can inspire moments of connection with God—while abstract thinkers can spend hours contemplating one of the attributes of God in the quietness of their own bedroom.

As an aside, however, I would be remiss not to mention the value of daily time alone with God every day—no matter who you are, how you think, or your personality type. For me, it helps so much to focus my thoughts on Him and His Word in the morning before I face the day's blessings *and* challenges. Then I can view and respond to them better. We're talking about the spiritual discipline of communicating with God. You don't have to decipher thought patterns and communication styles before tumbling your thoughts out to Him. He innately and intimately understands and relates to you because He made you. And you need to connect with Him every day in order to comprehend your world from His perspective and live the life for which He created you. Remember, *how* you choose to communicate with Him is up to your preferences, but be sure to do it!

TIME TOGETHER FOR THE TWO OF YOU

1. Compare your answers to the beginning quiz and discuss how you feel about the results.

2. Brainstorm a list of strengths the Abstract Thinker brings to your relationship, and then have that person share what makes communication difficult and what would make it easier.*

3. Brainstorm a list of strengths the Concrete Thinker brings to your relationship, and then have that person share what makes communication difficult and what would make it easier.*

4. Each of you answer this question: How do you communicate with God?

5. End your time together by having both of you pray—each thanking God for specific strengths found in this chapter that make your partner a good match for you.

*If one or both of you seem balanced between these extremes, you may want to skip question 2 and/or 3.

CHAPTER

7

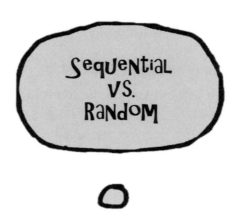

Sequential vs. Random

"How's the planning coming along?" Alex asked his wife, who sat at the table writing out invitations to their daughter's birthday party. "I'm sure Jen will love the theme—these cards are cute."

"*Oh, that reminds me,*" Karen said, jumping up and heading toward the kitchen. "Now that Jen's asleep, I can bring the party stuff in from the car and put it up in the attic."

Alex followed Karen out to the car to help. "How come you didn't bring the stuff in this afternoon before she came home from school?"

"I didn't really think about it." Karen hauled one big bag out of the trunk and handed it to Alex, then grabbed a second one and shut the trunk.

"When are you getting the cake?"

"Sometime tomorrow. I've got a list somewhere, but you know how I am. I'll just get it all done somehow. I'm more creative when I kick back and hang loose with the schedule." Karen shut the attic door and followed Alex down the steps to the kitchen again.

"I don't know how you do it. I follow my detailed list down to the minute. With you, I'm always surprised you don't miss things— but you generally manage to pull it off." He gave her an admiring glance. *"And you do everything with style!"*

Are you Sequential or Random Thinker?

▶ **You might make a list, but you do the items in a haphazard order.**

NOT AT ALL TRUE OF ME...............VERY TRUE OF ME
1 — 2 — 3 — 4 — 5 — 6 — 7 — 8 — 9 — 10

▶ **Your motto is: "Just get it done!"**

NOT AT ALL TRUE OF ME...............VERY TRUE OF ME
1 — 2 — 3 — 4 — 5 — 6 — 7 — 8 — 9 — 10

▶ **You like to try new ways to solve old problems.**

NOT AT ALL TRUE OF ME...............VERY TRUE OF ME
1 — 2 — 3 — 4 — 5 — 6 — 7 — 8 — 9 — 10

▶ **You don't like routine—you like to keep life fresh.**

NOT AT ALL TRUE OF ME...............VERY TRUE OF ME
1 — 2 — 3 — 4 — 5 — 6 — 7 — 8 — 9 — 10

▶ **Structure and order makes you feel boxed in and restless.**

NOT AT ALL TRUE OF ME...............VERY TRUE OF ME
1 — 2 — 3 — 4 — 5 — 6 — 7 — 8 — 9 — 10

▶ **People have been known to call you spontaneous and impulsive.**

NOT AT ALL TRUE OF ME...............VERY TRUE OF ME
1 — 2 — 3 — 4 — 5 — 6 — 7 — 8 — 9 — 10

Sequential thinkers will have the lower numbers, while random thinkers will have the higher numbers. If you scored a 10 or below, you are a very strong sequential thinker. If you scored between 45 and 50 you are a very random thinker. How did your partner score?

GOTTA KNOW INFO

How do you organize the information in your head? This is a question that drives homeschooling parents to my door to have me interview their children and find out what makes them tick—so the parent can teach them more effectively. For many years I used the same question to help identify whether the child was a sequential or random thinker: "When you make your bed every morning, do you always use the same steps or do you just get it done?" But sometime in the past twenty years, Americans stopped making their beds! Now I ask: "Do you follow basically the exact same routine when you wake up in the morning, or do you just get up and get ready for the day?" How about you?

The sequential thinker likes to take one detail at a time, in context, in order. And once the person finds a good method by which to accomplish a routine task, the same steps are generally followed every time. On the other hand, the random thinker just gets it done, not caring if the same steps were followed or not. The important thing is the task being completed.

Looking back at the personality section, we can compare the sequential thinkers with the Cholerics and Melancholies. In fact, if you are a Choleric/Melancholy mix, you are almost certain to be very sequential. On the flip side, the Sanguine/Phlegmatic mix will generally think in a more relaxed way. This random thinker may seem more scatterbrained, but astonishingly, the task usually gets done—and sometimes with greater flair.

Good News

The strengths in this chapter cannot be divided into two equal sections, because it is when the sequential and random thinkers get together and share their ideas on a project that the rich rewards show up. Think of the random thinker as the right side of the brain (the side that is inventive and creative) and the sequential thinker as the left side (the part that organizes and uses what the right side produces). We need both sides of our brain to function well in the world—just like a couple who wants to solve problems together must utilize and respect what both members bring to the relationship. Although a human is capable of using both sides of the brain, one side will be dominant.

Challenging News

It's easy to say that we should appreciate our differences, but in real life, it takes *work*. It is so much easier to wish they processed, thought, and came to conclusions just the way you do. Take heart and take your frustrations to the Lord—He knows you both best and will help you work together.

Traits of the Sequential Thinker:

▶ Thinks line by line, step-by-step
▶ Uses a logical train of thought
▶ Conversation is easy to follow
▶ Has a plan and sticks to it
▶ Makes lists and follows the items in order

Traits of the Random Thinker:

▶ Chunks information (no particular sequence)
▶ May be able to skip mental steps and still arrive at correct conclusion
▶ May seem impulsive or spontaneous
▶ Appears not to have a plan—they just get it done
▶ May make a list but rarely follows points in order

THE GOD FACTOR

It's easy to see God as a sequential thinker. After all, look around at His perfectly ordered world. Even the moon plays a part in the ebb and flow of the tides, and the earth rotates on a precise schedule.

Is a random thinker, then, an unnatural part of God's world? As a random thinker myself, I've struggled with this question and come to the conclusion that God is both sequential and random, at least in our eyes. For example, there are times when random thinkers' minds just skip a step or two, but they come to the same conclusion as the sequential thinkers. It reminds me of running up the stairs two at a time—some people can do it, others can't. And certainly some situations require precise steps—like a science experiment where one missed segment of the directions can throw off the desired result. But I think God's mind can skip steps since He knows all the outcomes already. He has the power to accomplish His will in any order He wants. He has a plan and somehow works everything (even what looks chaotic to us) together for good (Jeremiah 29:11; Romans 8:28).

COMMUNICATING TOGETHER
Communicating with the Sequential Thinker

▶ Be as logical as possible
▶ Don't bounce from topic to topic without warning
▶ Appreciate their plan, discuss it, and then stick to it
  if working together
▶ Give yourself permission to *not* be like this person, but
  cooperate with them

> ### Praying for My Sequential Thinker
>
> *Thank You* for this organized, methodical thinker. *Help me remember* to carefully structure my thinking when we are working together so I do not frustrate _____. Help me to think in a more logical way when we are trying to communicate.

When working together, remember the sequential person needs a list, needs steps, and a logical path to the desired outcome. If the two of you are poles apart (*very* sequential and *very* random), try separating tasks so that you fulfill your responsibilities in your random way and express yourself creatively, but the other person will have a list of practical things to take care of and feel secure about knowing and checking off.

Communicating with the Random Thinker

▶ Try to understand that random thinking is not wrong thinking, just different
▶ Remind the person to be logical with you as much as possible
▶ Don't push your lists or ordered processes on this free thinker
▶ Appreciate the creative ideas that flow from them

[
Praying **for My Random Thinker**

Thank You for this wild, zany, creative thinker. *Help me remember* to be nonjudgmental and patient. Remind me to trust _____ for the final product. When we work together, help me to follow a different train of thought or at least not be frustrated when I am unable to do so.
]

A sequential person accommodating a random thinker has more of a challenge than the random person trying to connect with the sequential thinker. The reason for this is because the random person practices being sequential every day because the world demands it—computers, cookbooks, dictionaries, etc. Furthermore, society as a whole does not fully appreciate (or understand) the random thinker and pressures that person into conforming to a sequential lifestyle. Think about it: no sane person is going to run errands haphazardly—not with today's gas prices! So know that you have a difficult, maybe impossible job ahead of you, to try to understand your random thinker's mind. Really all you need to do is cut them some slack, allowing for differences as long as the person is not shirking their responsibilities. Appreciate the random thinker's creativity, outside-the-box thinking, and unique perspective. And pray for patience and compassion.

&

Talk Easy Listen Hard

TIME TOGETHER FOR THE TWO OF YOU

1. Compare your answers to the beginning quiz and discuss how you feel about the results.

2. Brainstorm a list of strengths the Sequential Thinker brings to your relationship, and then have that person share what makes communication difficult and what would make it easier.*

3. Brainstorm a list of strengths the Random Thinker brings to your relationship, and then have that person share what makes communication difficult and what would make it easier.*

4. End your time together by having both of you pray— each thanking God for specific strengths found in this chapter that make your partner a good match for you.

*If one or both of you seem balanced between these extremes, you may want to skip question 2 and/or 3.

@

CHAPTER

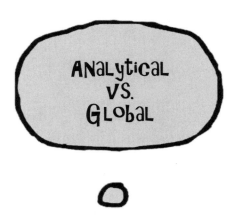

ANaLyticaL vS. GLobaL

Brad turned the corner and shifted gears as he asked Gina, "So what did you enjoy most about the Simmons' party tonight?"

"*I loved those* little spiral cookies on the buffet table. Oh, and I've never seen such wonderful decorations on a tree," Gina replied. "I also liked the way the stockings were handmade with the intricate sewing and beading. That must have taken forever."

"Wow, I didn't even notice the stockings. They were by the fireplace, I assume?"

Gina laughed. "Yep, hung with care. Did you notice the interesting taste of the mulled cider? I just can't put my finger on what was in it." She turned toward him, "So, what did you notice?"

Brad laughed, "Not the same things as you, that's for sure. I don't know how you can be in one place for such a short time and remember so many details! I hung out with a couple of the guys from work, and we talked pretty much the whole time." He turned the corner onto their street. "I guess I just noticed that the house was beautifully decorated for Christmas and all the Simmons—even the children—were warm and welcoming."

"Hey, before I forget," Gina changed the subject, "did you think any more about the summer missions trip to Mexico City?"

Brad nodded. "Yeah. I really think we should do it. It's a great opportunity to stretch ourselves beyond our comfort zone and also find out if God might be leading us into full-time ministry like that."

"Whoa, buddy!" Since they'd reached home and Brad put the car in park, Gina took off her seat belt and turned to face him. "Don't sign us up until we know all the details. We don't know the duration of the trip, or exactly where we would be going. I just don't think we should make a decision until we know more."

Brad frowned. "I just feel like it's a really great idea."

Gina crossed her arms. "But we don't know the details!"

"It seems like a great fit for our interests, our abilities, and our desire to serve the Lord."

"We don't even know the dates."

"Relax, Gina. We're not signing our lives away—it's a summer missions trip. Try looking at the big picture, hon."

"Oh, Brad, you make me crazy! The trip doesn't make sense to me because I just don't have enough data yet."

Are you an Analytical or Global Thinker?

▶ **In school, I was better at writing essays than remembering lots of facts.**

NOT AT ALL TRUE OF ME..................VERY TRUE OF ME
1 — 2 — 3 — 4 — 5 — 6 — 7 — 8 — 9 — 10

▶ **I sometimes read the last page of a book first so I know what's going to happen.**

NOT AT ALL TRUE OF ME..................VERY TRUE OF ME
1 — 2 — 3 — 4 — 5 — 6 — 7 — 8 — 9 — 10

▶ **I love the give-and-take of working on a project with a whole group of people.**

NOT AT ALL TRUE OF ME................VERY TRUE OF ME
1 — 2 — 3 — 4 — 5 — 6 — 7 — 8 — 9 — 10

▶ **In a questionable or debatable situation, I generally trust my gut instincts and feelings.**

NOT AT ALL TRUE OF ME................VERY TRUE OF ME
1 — 2 — 3 — 4 — 5 — 6 — 7 — 8 — 9 — 10

▶ **People come to me for help with problems, because I can generally see the big picture.**

NOT AT ALL TRUE OF ME................VERY TRUE OF ME
1 — 2 — 3 — 4 — 5 — 6 — 7 — 8 — 9 — 10

▶ **I enjoy philosophizing and discussing theories with friends.**

NOT AT ALL TRUE OF ME................VERY TRUE OF ME
1 — 2 — 3 — 4 — 5 — 6 — 7 — 8 — 9 — 10

▶ **I am flexible, usually go with the flow, and can do several things at once.**

NOT AT ALL TRUE OF ME................VERY TRUE OF ME
1 — 2 — 3 — 4 — 5 — 6 — 7 — 8 — 9 — 10

Analytical thinkers will have the lower numbers, while global thinkers will have the higher numbers. If you scored a 10 or below, you have very strong tendencies to think analytically. If you scored between 45 and 50 you see things from a global perspective. How did your partner score?

GOTTA KNOW INFO

The detail-oriented, focused analytical thinker gets just as frustrated with the spontaneous, concept-driven global thinker— and vice versa. Yet these two types of people bring balance to a relationship if they can just learn to respect each other's needs and value each other's strengths.

Analytical vs. Global

Couples who don't realize that it is possible to come to solutions from these two angles can become hostile with each other or refuse to work together. They can be under the assumption that their partner's thinking is inferior to their own, or that the partner is deliberately trying to be difficult. Seeking to work together brings great rewards.

Good News

Analytical thinkers like things ordered in a step-by-step manner. They pay close attention to details and generally like to focus on one thing at time. Their memory is very specific and they give direct, factual answers. They look at situations objectively and honestly. The analytical thinker is self-motivated, logical, and often meticulous.

On the other hand, global thinkers bring to the discussion a sense of the overall purpose. They have the ability to stand back and see the big picture. Very relationship driven, they enjoy working with others in a group where many options and possibilities can be discussed and worked through. Sensitive to body language and moods, they can often read between the lines. If they can't prove a theory, they may make a decision based on how they feel about it. These people are highly flexible and creative.

Challenging News

Analytical thinkers find the facts but can sometimes miss the main idea. They rarely risk becoming personally or emotionally involved, preferring to keep to the perceived safety of logical, black-and-white facts. Because of this, analytical thinkers are slow to make decisions.

Don't ask analytical thinkers to perform or produce something unexpected—they play by the rules. They like to be thoroughly prepared, knowing what is expected so they are assured success in every detail. And please don't ask them to do a second task before the first one is completed to their liking.

The global thinkers, however, enjoy a break in the routine. But these flexible thinkers can feel absolutely lost if you don't give

Talk Easy Listen Hard

them the main goal or basic topic of the discussion. If they don't have the overview clear in their minds, they have nothing to hold together all the details flying at them—and they lose them. They won't retain pieces of information if they don't have a general idea of what you're talking about. It's almost like the global thinker takes the whole and dissects it, while the analytical thinker wants to add all the pieces together and come to a conclusion.

A global thinker often feels uncomfortable around analytical thinkers who demand facts when the global thinker just has a gut feeling. Global thinkers take criticism personally, and can be very unproductive and despondent without appropriate reassurance and encouragement.

Traits of the Analytical Thinker:

▶ Pays close attention to and remembers details and facts
▶ Sometimes misses the overall main idea or general concept
▶ Very objective and cognitive
▶ Prefers to focus on and finish one thing at a time
▶ Likes things ordered logically
▶ Believes there is a *best* way to do something
▶ Rarely becomes emotionally involved; is detached
▶ Sees things very black-and-white with a strong sense of justice

Traits of the Global Thinker:

▶ Keys in on people and relationships
▶ Remembers concepts; sees the big picture
▶ Subjective and aware of feelings; reads body language
▶ Good at multitasking; can keep many balls in the air at one time
▶ Goes with the flow; is flexible
▶ Sees many options and the different ways to do something
▶ Works well with others, appreciates praise, and takes criticism personally
▶ Gracious, encouraging, and complimentary to others

THE GOD FACTOR

God is a perfect blend of analytic and global processing. He has a grand plan, but is personally involved with the tiniest details. He is relational, but also direct, just, and objective.

We can trust Him to bring us together in unity, valuing each other's strengths and filling in for each other's weaknesses. Is it any wonder that God designed us in this way?

He is the only one who can give us the wisdom and perseverance to work together effectively. He receives glory when His children display the unity of heart, purpose, and mind talked about in Philippians 2:1–4.

COMMUNICATING TOGETHER
Communicating with the Analytical Thinker

▶ Remember this person thinks in black-and-white, right and wrong
▶ Try to be logical and factual in your delivery
▶ Give them time to process the situation alone when possible
▶ Keep this person focused on the big picture
▶ Help this person pay attention to people, not just the project
▶ Appreciate this person's attention to detail and memory
▶ If time or patience is in short supply, stick to the facts

> ### Praying for My Analytical Thinker
>
> *Thank You* for _____'s attention to details and ability to retain facts and data. *Help me remember* to appreciate these qualities and ask for the big picture if it is not shared it at the beginning of our conversation.

Help your analytical thinker understand the purpose and expectations for a given conversation (or activity) as well as time to think and prepare whenever possible. Then try not to change gears too suddenly or dramatically in the middle of things.

Where the global thinker wants the overview first, the analytical thinker needs you to present the details in a logical order before you arrive at a conclusion. An analytical thinker feels uncomfortable with generalities until the details have been fleshed out. So don't expect that person to make personal application or draw conclusions too early in the game. Also, if possible, exhaust one concept before moving on to the next thought.

Be brief and factual with the analytical thinker; avoid a long explanation when a simple yes or no will do. When expressing an opinion, state it as such so the other person doesn't mistake your idea as desired fact.

Communicating with the Global Thinker

▶ Remember this person *feels* things deeply; keep comments positive when possible
▶ Relax and go with the flow as much as you are able
▶ Be available as a sounding board
▶ Don't recite a list of facts without first presenting the main concept
▶ Help this person focus on the project details, not just the human element
▶ Appreciate their ability to see the overall concept and outline
▶ Under a time deadline, start with a general *what* and *why*

[

Praying for My Global Thinker

Thank You for this big-picture thinker. *Help me remember* to present the general idea, goal, or main questions at the beginning of our conversation. Give me patience when _____ can't remember facts that seem so important to me. Help me be gentle and forgiving when issuing reminders.

]

To best communicate with a global thinker, reverse the above tips. Herein lies the challenge for a married couple who find themselves in both camps.

The global thinker hates having to give an analytical, step-by-step explanation—or even worse, not having a chance to give any explanation. Give this person the opportunity—and encouragement—to share their feelings about the topic. Yes, I said *feelings* because that's what they really want to share. Not the facts, but how the facts work together and relate to the person's life. And give credit where credit is due. To a global thinker who is overly sensitive to criticism, praise and encourage where possible for maximum creativity and overall success.

Not knowing the desired end frustrates a global thinker so greatly they usually miss most of the details in between the beginning and the end and must go back and rethink. Whenever possible, outline the topic first and give an idea where you want the conversation to go and where it will possibly end. *Then* you can turn your global thinker loose!

TIME TOGETHER FOR THE TWO OF YOU

1. Compare your answers to the beginning quiz and discuss how you feel about the results.

2. Brainstorm a list of strengths the Analytical Thinker brings to your relationship, and then have that person share what makes communication difficult and what would make it easier.*

3. Brainstorm a list of strengths the Global Thinker brings to your relationship, and then have that person share what makes communication difficult and what would make it easier.*

4. End your time together by having both of you pray— each thanking God for specific strengths found in this chapter that make your partner a good match for you.

If one or both of you seem balanced between these extremes, you may want to skip question 2 and/or 3.

PART THREE

Love Languages--
How We Communicate Our Feelings

In the 1990s, author Gary Chapman introduced the concept of love languages to Christian readers. These groundbreaking ideas about common expressions of love caused us to think consciously about how we give and receive love. He made a case for understanding our different preferences and learning to love smarter.

This explained to me why Rich seems to need me to *do* things for him, and why he gets so frustrated with me and tunes me out when I leave the laundry sitting in the drier. It also reveals why I feel devastated when he doesn't want to talk to me or doesn't say "I love you" enough for my liking.

So what are the five love languages? We give and receive love through: *touch, words, gifts, acts of service,* and *quality time.*

As you analyze yourself and your partner in light of these languages, look for an order of preference. If you could only have one of the five types of love, which would it be? What would take second place, and third? If this becomes difficult, ask yourself which one you could live without—which is of *least* importance. Try to order them by preference from one to five, one being the highest priority—it's okay to have a tie! Don't forget to record this information in appendix A.

Notable Quotables

"The Christian faith is meant to be lived moment by moment. It isn't some broad, general outline— it's a long walk with a real Person. Details count: passing thoughts, small sacrifices, a few encouraging words, little acts of kindness, brief victories over nagging sins."

Joni Eareckson Tada

Two words of caution. First, people don't always give and receive in the same language—although you can generally look at the way a person *demonstrates* love and know their receiving language. If you are not sure of your partner's love language and you can't easily talk about it, try speaking primarily one language each week. Observe your loved one's reactions over the five week trial.

Second, this information can be dangerous if used in reverse—fight any urge to withhold love from your partner. And if you realize your partner is using a love language *against* you, bring it out into the open and discuss it if possible. It may be unintentional.

Finally, consider the fact that God, the author of love, is fluent in all five languages. He desires to help the two of you understand yourselves and love each other effectively. Ask Him right now for revelation as you read the last five chapters of this book.

CHAPTER

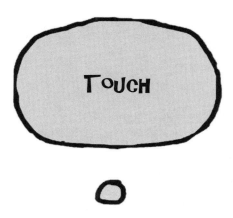

TOUCH

The scales confirmed what Alice already knew: she needed to lose some weight. After getting dressed, she completed household chores in the bedrooms until she heard Ted's car pull out of the garage. He wouldn't want to hug me anyway, she reasoned, but he'd do it anyway out of habit.

Over the next several weeks, Alice wore baggier clothing and tried to ward off any of Ted's attempts to be affectionate—which wasn't an easy feat. He playfully tried nipping the back of her neck while she was washing dishes. She avoided him by leaning over to wipe at a spot on the floor. At church, he slid his arm around her shoulders during the church service. She endured this until one time she leaned forward and his hand slid down and grazed her love handles. That touch made her feel so uncomfortable, she actually got up in the middle of the service to visit the ladies' room. Most recently she pleaded a headache when he made a few playfully suggestive remarks out of earshot of the children.

Now she felt bad, and Ted seemed to be growing distant. Had he stayed at work longer in the evenings of this past week? Was he just reflecting her bad mood caused by her poor self-image? What should she do?

Anybody Need Touch?

▶ I greet almost everyone with a hug or
warm handshake. ....YES or NO

▶ When talking to people, I often reach out
and touch them. ....YES or NO

▶ I don't need a large area of personal space, I like to be
close to people. ....YES or NO

▶ I'm known for giving great back rubs or
playful tickles. ....YES or NO

▶ I love to daydream and replay my sweetheart's
kisses during the day. ....YES or NO

▶ I'll do almost anything for you if you snuggle
with me or play with my hair. ....YES or NO

GOTTA KNOW INFO

Does your partner often hold your hand? When the two of you watch television together, does she snuggle up to you on the couch? Does he play with your hair or kiss the back of your neck when you are not making love? Does she hug and kiss you before leaving the house? Does he invite you to enjoy a massage—or ask you to rub his back before he goes to sleep?

Notice I didn't ask if the person initiates sex on a regular basis! The love language of touch includes the sexual relationship, but is certainly not limited to it. A host of physical, sensory delights far exceed (in number) the joys of physical union.

The love language of touch includes hand-holding, kissing, hugging, holding, patting, stroking, sitting close, snuggling —anything that involves body-to-body contact.

While it is true that certain love languages can be matched up with particular personalities, this is not always the case. Where touch is concerned, the people-oriented Phlegmatics and Sanguines probably enjoy touching more than the practical, efficient Cholerics and Melancholies. But don't let this deter you from learning to enjoy a positive, loving touch from your sweetheart!

The Good News

By this time, almost everyone has heard stories about children deprived of physical affection and touching early in their lives. Touch helps us develop physically, mentally, emotionally, spiritually, and socially. It is a *connection* that helps us emotionally bond with each other and gives us a sense of security and belonging.

Especially for Men:
Touch does not equal sex—but can lead to it!

Guys, please don't forget the simple romantic touches women crave—especially if your wife's love language is touch. Discipline yourself to make little loving touches a habitual part of your everyday relationship, and your sex life will benefit. Because men are microwaves and women are slow pressure cookers in the world of sexual fulfillment, you can boost your wife's interest in sex if you keep her attention between sessions of lovemaking. The key is focusing on delighting her during everyday romantic moments —rather than looking too far ahead to the coming passion and missing the connection of a simple shared moment.

The human body, created with a central nervous system, uses the brain to send and receive messages through an amazing number of nerve endings. In our fast-paced, task-oriented world, most of the messages sent to our brains are superseded by "important" thinking. God exemplified and commanded a period of rest for each week. The more obvious purpose for this command includes

HELP!

I'm not a touchy-feely person.

Remember that different is okay!

God doesn't wire everyone the same. Because He has placed you in a partnership with someone who does like to be touched, God is the first one to ask for help. The next step is to be honest with your mate and explain how you feel, while reaffirming your love and commitment to the relationship. And just because you don't enjoy touch doesn't mean you have to simply endure it. Recondition your mind, by God's grace, to see this as a way to bless your spouse, and then *just do it* and allow God to give you appropriate feelings.

coming away from the world to focus clearly on our Creator and Savior. Another key opportunity results from a weekly rest time: when we shut down our cognitive thinking, and then sensory delights that have been ignored all week can be enjoyed.

For example, turn your palm up to expose the inside part of your forearm, close your eyes to eliminate distractions so you can concentrate, and then very gently run your fingertips or fingernails up and down that small section of your arm. Of course, this is much more effective when done by someone you love—but you can get the idea of a relaxing, pleasant, physical-yet-emotional reaction. The endorphins released in your body by the gentle, tickling sensation tell your body to relax and be happy.

The Challenging News

Because what is *inside* an individual is often represented by their *outside* appearance, our bodies play an integral role in upkeep of our self-esteem. How other people see us matters to us. But sometimes we perceive ourselves differently than the rest of the world. We get hung up on how we think we should look, or how we perceive someone else wants us to look.

People who are discontent with their bodies tend to overprotect them and minimize anything relating to them—including touch. If your own primary love language is touch, your need for love may transcend this obstacle. If touch is not high on your list, just a general awareness of its importance to your mate may be enough to help you love them more effectively.

Even if you have a beautiful body, touch can be a problem. If you naturally dislike touch, something as simple as bumping into your sweetie in an enclosed area could make you feel uncomfortable. In fact, on some days it might even irritate you.

All of us—without exception—have an internal radar device that alerts us when someone invades our personal space. If someone gets too close to that invisible line, we tense up. When the line is crossed we feel violated. Because personal space is defined by each individual, it provides more reason to study each other and learn how to communicate in each other's languages.

Another problem with touching can be directly related to touches from your childhood. If you grew up in an affectionate, loving home where touch was an acceptable way to express love for each other you were blessed. Many of today's adults grew up in dysfunctional homes where touching was either nonexistent or it was hurtful. Learning to process through bad touching and get to the point of enjoying loving touches can be a long, hard road and may even require godly counseling to help move the two of you to a place of healing and normalcy.

THE GOD FACTOR

Think for a moment about what it must have been like when Jesus walked the earth. Examine the instances recorded in Scripture when Jesus touched a man or woman—even the children. (Matthew 4:24; 8:14-15; 14:35-36; 17:6-7; 19:14-15). What was His touch like?

What does *your* touch feel like to your partner? Is God healing battered emotions as you hold them in your arms for a long hug? Do you demonstrate the warmth of God's unconditional and reconciling love—even when the other person doesn't deserve it? How easy it is to pull away, to withdraw physically from someone who hurts or frustrates us. But, by giving and receiving forgiveness, the gap can be closed. And through your being close by and offering loving touch, you nurture the inner person too.

At this time in our lives and in God's plan for the world, He is Spirit. We are flesh. How can you be God's hands and meet the

z-z-z

physical needs of the person you and God so dearly love?

Luke 7:36-50 tells the story of the woman who touched Jesus' feet, washing them with her tears, anointing them with oil, and wiping them with her hair. When was the last time you touched your sweetheart's feet or did some other physical ministry to bless them?

[
Praying for My Sweetheart

Thank You for this affectionate, hands-on person. *Help me remember* to touch _____. Help me learn to be gentle and kind when communicating a need for space when I don't feel like being touched. Make me more touch oriented!
]

A HAPPY ENDING

Alice happened to come across *The Five Love Languages* in a local Christian bookstore. She began analyzing her and Ted's individual preferences. Even before she completed the book, she designed a plan to test her theories about Ted and his love languages. On the first day of her plan, she worked all day to prepare Ted's favorite meal for dinner, made sure the house just sparkled, and put on an outfit he always seemed to compliment. She called him at work to invite him to come home as early as possible to relax and spend some time together.

From the moment he walked into the house and she greeted him with a kiss and hug, Alice watched closely to see what he noticed first and anything that drew a response. When he didn't let go of her at the front door but led her over to the couch, she spied her first clue.

After she placed his dinner in front of him and hesitated for a moment behind his chair to massage his shoulders and kiss the back of his neck, his audible sigh confirmed another clue. After dinner, he elected to help her with the dishes—turning back the clock to the more carefree time when they'd chased each other around the kitchen and acted goofy.

Talk Easy Listen Hard

Although Alice's specially planned night ended with lovemaking, Ted confided in her just before they fell asleep, "I've missed touching your beautiful body."

"Oh, Ted, how can you say that—I really need to lose weight." Alice was thankful the darkness hid her embarrassment.

Ted turned toward her and tenderly wrapped her into his arms. "I'm not perfect. You're not perfect. That makes us a perfect pair."

TIME TOGETHER FOR THE TWO OF YOU

1. Consider the following scale, ranging from one (1) "I almost never want touch" to five (5) "being touched really makes me feel loved." One at a time, share where you'd rank this love language and explain your choice.

2. If you chose a four (4) or five (5) on the scale, tell your partner of the most recent times when you felt loved because of touch. Then offer other suggestions on ways your partner can express love in this language, or mention some of the fifty-two suggestions below that you find appealing.

If you are reading alone without the interaction of your partner, think back over the past few days and ask yourself if they showed love to you in this language. If so, was it often? Over the next few days, deliberately show love in this language (but cutting back on the others for this short experiment)— and observe how your partner responds. Of course, the more straight-forward discovery method is directly asking!

52

WAYS TO USE

Touch

to EXPRESS
Your Love:

1 Hand-holding
2 Kissing
3 Hugging
4 Holding
5 Patting
6 Arm around shoulder
7 Head on shoulder
8 Tickling
9 Back rub
10 Shoulder rub
11 Scalp massage
12 Playing with hair
13 Facial massage
14 Foot massage
15 Hand massage
16 Body massage
17 Nuzzling
18 Back scratching
19 Hair brushing
20 Nudging
21 Giving a peck on the cheek
22 Embracing
23 Cuddling
24 Playing footsie
25 Leaning
26 Sitting close

27 Covering eyes to surprise
28 Tousling hair
29 High five
30 Sitting on lap
31 Dancing
32 Lying side-by-side
33 Spooning
34 Eskimo kissing
35 Nibbling
36 Playing with ears
37 Cheek to cheek
38 Washing feet
39 Linking arms
40 Holding their arm
41 Helping out of the car
42 Interlacing fingers
43 Piggyback riding
44 Wrestling
45 Playing Twister
46 Tracing with fingertips
47 Games involving touch
48 Caressing
49 Shaving those prickles
50 Stroking
51 Snuggling
52 Light, feathery touches

Talk Easy Listen Hard

CHAPTER

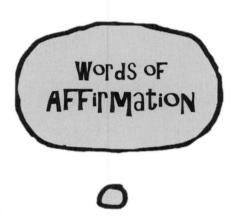

Words of AFFirMation

Stacey and Will sipped milk shakes in companionable silence in the ice-cream shop after the movie concluded.

"*I liked the movie. How about you?*" Stacey asked.

"'Course you liked it—it was a chick flick." He grinned at her.

"I love you for taking me to it. I hope you had fun too." She took another sip. "I love you." Silence. "I think we're a good fit for each other—we're so different." Sip. "I really love you." Silence, longer this time. Stacey couldn't help herself. She had to ask, "Don't you want to tell me you love me too?"

Will just looked at Stacey, and then said, "Hon, I think you say it enough for the two of us."

Crushed, Stacey blinked back tears, focused on her milk shake and mentally reassured herself that Will loved her—even if he didn't say it.

Do you Listen for Love?

▶ I enjoy giving and receiving compliments. ....YES or NO

▶ If I think my honey looks good, I'm quick to say so. ......YES or NO

▶ I feel taken for granted, when my thoughtfulness
isn't acknowledged. ....YES or NO

▶ I love it when I overhear my spouse speaking
well of me to someone else. ....YES or NO

▶ Before I go to bed, say good-bye, or hang up
the phone, I say, "I love you." ....YES or NO

▶ I never get tired of hearing, "I love you"
or "You're wonderful." ....YES or NO

GOTTA KNOW INFO

Words have the power to comfort or crush, soothe or slam, give hope or hold a person back. To some people, words mean everything. Their auditory receptors need to hear the truth as badly as the visual person needs to see it. Don't perceive this issue as the person manipulating you with a selfish need for compliments—they have an inner wiring that requires words.

What is the most recent compliment you've given your partner? Do you recall *any* praise you've doled out in the past? If your memory cannot produce answers, wake up! You need to open your mouth and use the gift of words to encourage and uplift that special person—and all of the people around you. We all need to hear words of affirmation.

Good News

You can make someone's day with the right words. Your words of confidence can inspire record-breaking achievements. Your

Talk Easy Listen Hard

understanding words can heal a wounded spirit. Your wise words can straighten out a misunderstanding. Your words of apology or forgiveness can restore your relationship. Thoughtful words can enrich, constructive criticism kindly spoken can motivate, and God's truth spoken to the heart of an anxious person can bring real peace.

Challenging News

Hurtful words can cut like a knife and leave lasting scars. My father still remembers his elementary teacher who belittled him with one scathing remark about his oral reading, and to this day he feels overwhelmed when reading in public. There are just as many ways to strike down a person with words as there are to build up and edify.

Notable Quotables

I realized a few years ago, as I studied my Sanguine nature, that I don't always talk to Rich for his benefit. Sometimes my talking centers completely around me and my projects, simply because I want to share my excitement. Other times I give Rich a piece of my mind in the middle of a heated discussion, because I think I need to let him know how I feel. But does he really want to know? Better question: Is he receptive right now—is he able to take in my ideas and process them? Or is now not the best time? I must work constantly on translating into his language (paying attention to timing, content, and presentation) and relying on the Holy Spirit to prompt me when I need to confront him. The two most important parts of my communication should be *motive* and *attitude* (Ephesians 4:15).

"Let your words be the genuine picture of your heart."

JOHN WESLEY

Sometimes talking too much waters down what you have to say to the point where the person isn't even listening anymore. Like the boy who cried wolf, you can dull the ears of your listener to the point of deafness. If you sound like a broken record, your spouse will eventually tune you out if they can't turn you off.

Another tip: refrain from simply saying what you think a person wants to hear. Don't embarrass and disrespect yourself in this way to score points—discontent about not telling the truth will often creep in. Be sincere. Be yourself. Discipline your tongue to speak honest, positive words of encouragement.

The Melancholy/Phlegmatics rarely experience my problem of saying too much, similar to the busy Choleric/Melancholies (for them the key is speaking *in love*). For these personality types, the most important communication tip is to liberally give words of encouragement. Stay positive. Compliment, affirm, and praise.

Praying **for My Sweetheart**

Thank You for this sensitive person. *Help me remember* to use my mouth to encourage, uplift, build up, support, praise, acknowledge, cheer, admire, celebrate, compliment, and honor. Help me to bring my complaints to You first, and then, if needed, in gentleness and love to _____ . Give me greater compassion so the words from my heart will be spoken in love and encouragement.

THE GOD FACTOR

Throughout the pages of the Bible, God continuously tells us of His love (John 3:16; Romans 8:35–39; Ephesians 3:16–19). The Father called Christ "The Word"—the living Word, God incarnate (John 1:1–18).

A few years ago, a Bible teacher took us to the creation story in Genesis 1. He pointed out that after the report of each day, God saw everything He made and pronounced it good. There is one notable exception to this repeated format. On day six when He created Adam and Eve, He broke the pattern in order to *talk* to them, before he pronounced the day and the creation of the day good. What a phenomenal privilege and honor—to talk to the God of the universe. Words are one of God's greatest gifts. Are you using your gift for the good of others and the glory of God? How can you bless your sweetheart today with words of encouragement and affirmation? "The tongue has the power of life and death, and those who love it will eat its fruit" (Proverbs 18:21).

A HAPPY ENDING

After leaving the ice cream shop and getting into the car, Will and Stacey sat quietly in the car. Will made no move to turn on the engine. Instead, he turned toward Stacey and took her hands in his. "I love you." He paused and then looked in her eyes. "I'm not good with words. You're the one who talks all the time." He put a finger on her lips, smiled, and shook his head. "I'm just teasing you."

Then he gently squeezed her hands between his. "I guess I never thought about how much you need to hear the words. I'm sorry."

By this time, tears were slipping down Stacey's cheeks. Will kissed them, surprised she still had not said a word but pleased to feel her body relax against his.

Then, to his astonishment, Stacey took off her seat belt, scooted closer, and put on the middle belt, snuggling against him like she did when they were dating. He chuckled. "I'm gonna have to learn to talk a little more in the future." Kissing the top of her head, he added a heartfelt, "I do love you, sweetheart."

TIME TOGETHER FOR THE TWO OF YOU

1. Consider the following scale, ranging from one (1) "I almost never need words of affirmation" to five (5) "words really make me feel loved." One at a time, share where you'd rank this love language and explain your choice.

2. If you chose a four (4) or five (5) on the scale, tell your partner of the most recent times when you felt loved because of words. Then offer other suggestions on ways your partner can express love in this language, or mention some of the fifty-two suggestions below that you find appealing.

If you are reading alone without the interaction of your partner, observe, experiment, or directly ask questions.

Talk Easy Listen Hard

52

WAYS TO USE

Words

to EXPRESS
Your Love:

1 "I love you."
2 "I love _____ about you."
3 "I appreciate the times you _____."
4 "I'm so glad God brought you into my life."
5 "I missed you."
6 "No one else _____s the way you do."
7 "I appreciate _____ about you."
8 "I hope our children inherit your _____."
9 "I couldn't have _____ without you."
10 "I LOVE YOU."
11 E-mailing
12 Sending a card
13 Writing a letter
14 Putting a sticky note somewhere fun
15 Writing in the sand at the beach
16 Renting a billboard
17 Lettering on a decorated cake
18 Using alphabet cereal or soup
19 Putting a note inside a fortune cookie
20 Putting a note in his truck
21 Tucking a note into her purse
22 Placing a few lines in the newspaper
23 Writing a poem
24 Personalized lyrics for her favorite song
25 Sing his favorite song to him
26 Composing a song

27 "How do you feel about _____?"
28 "I like the way you _____."
29 "You make me laugh when you _____."
30 "I like your _____."
31 "You are so good at _____."
32 "I'm glad you are _____."
33 "You make me feel _____."
34 "I love your _____."
35 "When you _____, I feel _____."
36 "You did a great job!"
37 Requesting a favorite song on radio
38 Complimenting in front of friends
39 Complimenting in front of family
40 Sending a telegram
41 Sending a message in a bottle
42 Writing in lipstick on the bathroom mirror
43 Putting a note in the lunch bag
44 Hiding notes in the house when you're away
45 Sharing a good book with notes in margins
46 Sharing a praise journal (each writes in it)
47 Sharing your diary entries
48 Reading a book together
49 Talking about the movie over coffee
50 Sharing your dreams and goals
51 Making New Year's resolutions together
52 Writing a story about the two of you

!

Love Language: Words of Affirmation

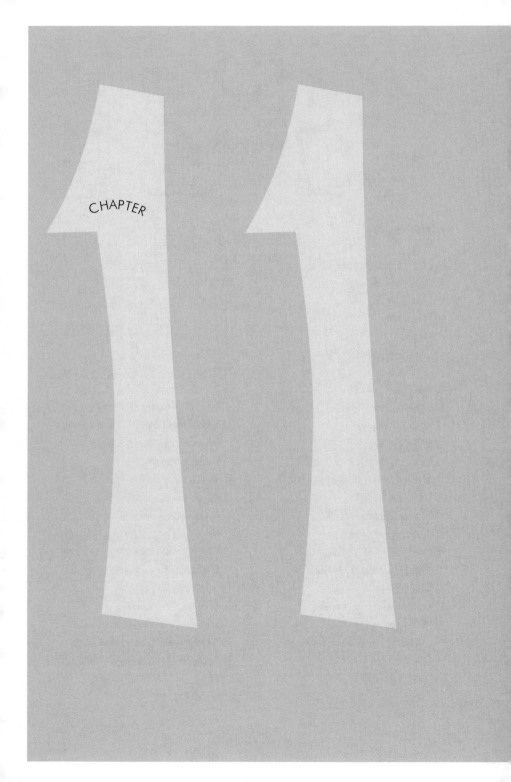

CHAPTER

Loving Gifts

Bryce looked up when he realized someone was standing at the opening of his cubicle. Lucky he was between calls. "Can I help you?" he asked the guy awkwardly holding a vase of flowers.

"These are for you." The fellow extended the arrangement and looked eager to be going.

"I . . . ah," Bryce stammered.

"They're for a Bryce Miller and that's you, right?" The guy glanced at the nameplate on the outside of the partition.

Bryce took the flowers. "Ah, yeah. Thanks." And the man disappeared as fast as he'd arrived. Then Bryce noticed the little card tucked into the blooms. He pulled it out as Joe, his closest coworker popped his head into Bryce's area.

"Pretty flowers. From the little woman?" Joe wiggled his eyebrows. "Or some secret admirer?"

"Hey, they're from my wife." His smile turned to a frown. "But we've been trying to cut costs lately. Why in the world would she go to the expense of a florist?"

Joe ventured closer and peered at the arrangement. "The fellow that dropped them off looks like one of the maintenance guys on the third floor. And it's not wrapped up in that fancy paper with a florist's sticker. Do you see a sticker anywhere?" They both looked over the cute, rather masculine arrangement of flowers.

"Nope, I don't see one."

Joe nodded. "See, I'll bet she didn't spend a bundle on them— but what a nice idea. Enjoy!" On his way out he turned back to ask, "Is today a special occasion?"

"No, I don't think so." Bryce sank into his chair, staring at the fragrant flowers. "We didn't fight. I didn't do anything spectacular lately. She gives me little stuff every once in a while for no apparent reason. But this is a little unusual—even for Jamie."

"Ever heard of the love languages, *pal?" Joe asked, and made himself a little more comfortable leaning against the inside wall of Bryce's cubicle.*

Do You Need Visual Symbols of Love?

▶ You enjoy spending great thought and energy
   on gifts for people you love. ....YES or NO

▶ You love to be surprised with flowers. ....YES or NO

▶ You look forward to Christmas shopping. ....YES or NO

▶ You think birthdays should last a whole week
   with a little gift every day. ....YES or NO

▶ The price of a gift doesn't matter to you—
   it's the thought that counts. ....YES or NO

▶ You try to always bring gifts for those hosting you
   in their homes. ....YES or NO

> You have a store of little gifts to give out if
> someone gives you something. ....YES or NO

Gotta Know Info

It's the thought that counts. This mantra fits the love language of gifts. The person who speaks and receives love through gifts understands that the price tag doesn't matter. It is all about the love that motivates the gift.

If your sweetheart speaks the language of gifts, you may have received an assortment of tangible expressions of their love over the years. Give back. Give of yourself. Use your talents to create things, your money to buy things, as well as your time and your energy. On a practical note, if this is your partner's primary love language, you might actually need to put an extra category into your budget so you can afford to give without feeling a pinch in the pocketbook.

The Good News

Probably the biggest benefit of gifts is their tangible permanence. Gifts, unlike the other expressions of love, generally last a lot longer and can be seen and touched. Can you remember your favorite gifts? Rich bought me a leather coat one Christmas, and as I enjoy it over and over again every winter I think of him.

Gifts don't need to be costly. Sometimes the simplest, handmade card touches a soft spot in the other person's

True Story

Rich and I were married in late May. My September birthday rolled around first, and he took me to a fancy restaurant for dinner, presented me with a long-stemmed rose, and gave me a beautiful card declaring his undying love. But I wondered, where was the party? Where was the crowd of well-wishers? I'd show him just how to celebrate a birthday when his January birthday arrived. Sure enough, I made sure the Mexican restaurant staff clapped and sang as they presented his dessert, and then we went home to a surprise party in our apartment—with the kids from his youth group. (Note to self: the youth were his job, not his buddies!) His comment to me after the last person left: "Please don't ever plan a surprise party for me again." The moral of this story: choose a gift or celebration in keeping with the preferences and tastes of the recipient.

heart—and that card can be cherished and saved forever. Another inexpensive gift could be your husband's favorite special-occasion soda from the grocery store (not something you buy every week, but once in a while an appreciated splurge of an extra dollar or two). In this chapter's opening story, Jamie bought an inexpensive bunch of flowers at the market and made the arrangement herself. Then she took it to her husband's office building and asked someone she found in the lobby to help her surprise him with them.

The benefit of buying a greeting card for your sweetie is not having to come up with the words yourself. There is a vast assortment of professionally written sentiments to fit the occasion. Your loved one can hardly protest a thoughtful, lasting gift costing under five dollars.

Simple is good. The more simple and inexpensive you keep your gifts, the more you can give. Simplify your life too. It is perfectly fine to write a reminder into your appointment book every week to give something special. Don't think of it as cold and calculating; it is better to remember than forget for long periods of time. The appointment book and the gift itself are insignificant compared to the importance of focusing on the other person. You are saying, by way of a tangible gift, "I love you."

Challenging News

Certain protests are common when it comes to this love language:

I don't have enough money to buy a nice gift. If you define a nice gift as something over five dollars, you still don't understand that the price tag is not important to a person who loves gifts—it's the thought that went into choosing or making the gift. The gift is not a measure of your love, rather it is an indication of your love. Do something creative with the little bit of resources you can muster.

I'm not creative. Find a friend who does have a creative streak and enlist help. God made each of us different than the next person —so find someone with whom you can swap talents and create something meaningful for your spouse. Your gift doesn't need to be perfect—some of my favorite objects sit on my kitchen windowsill, including several creative clay attempts by my daughter before she was old enough to be a consummate artist.

I hate to shop. Don't think of buying a gift as shopping. You needn't go to the mall and wander around aimlessly while people laden with shopping bags run into you and roll strollers over your toes. Yuck! Call your sweetheart's best friend and ask them to *secretly* help you brainstorm a list of little goodies and where to find them (if you hint around, maybe the person will even give you some help collecting the stuff). Amass a small collection of gifts and hide them away where they won't be found. Then you're set for a few weeks or months—maybe even a year—of gift-giving fun. Of course, since it's the thought that counts, a spontaneous gift or spur-of-the-moment item is also special.

Little knickknacks seem so trivial. Remember your loved one will treasure that the gift is from you or appreciate its association with something dear or a good memory. For example, the next time you do something special together, see if you can find a souvenir as a tangible reminder of the event. For example, if you go to New York City for the Macy's Thanksgiving Day Parade and your spouse drags you three blocks from your place in line to get a cup of coffee only to find you can't get back to your blanket without walking back five blocks, across and up two, get her a coffee cup ornament for Christmas to remind her of your love and the good laugh you shared after you found the rest of your group!

What if my gift isn't appreciated? A giver might not always get the reaction they hoped for. Has your sweetheart ever disapproved of a gift? Perhaps they thought your gift was too pricey or inappropriate in some other way. A friend of mine told me giving gifts to his wife has become so tricky, at major holidays he now just gives her money to spend. Money is nice, no argument there. But this utilitarian gift defeats the purpose of carefully choosing a gift to demonstrate your love.

GIFTS AND THE PERSONALITIES

Gifts is the one love language that does not seem to fit any one or two specific personality types. Therefore, let's take a look at how each personality uniquely uses this language of love:

Sanguines enjoy giving outrageous, fun, extravagant gifts—and they love to surprise the recipient. They often over-give, either in value or amount of gifts. By the time Christmas rolls around, I've collected so many gifts for Rich that both his stocking and the floor under the tree are overflowing with colorfully wrapped boxes and packages.

Cholerics tend to give practical, utilitarian gifts they often pick up at the last minute. They are likely to have the store wrap the gift for them or buy a gift card. Rich loves to pick up the phone and call a florist who will take his credit card and deliver his gift and message. Very efficient!

Melancholies give well-thought-out, often romantic gifts. They worry—it's in their nature—about the gift being just right for the person and the occasion! My mother fusses and fusses over giving my dad a fat Christmas stocking. She looks for things all year long that will be just perfect for him. She thinks about his hobbies and interests and finds the most delightful, thoughtful, useful gifts.

Phlegmatics also opt to let the store wrap the gift for them—saves time and energy! In recent years my father has sent me out to do his shopping for Mom. He hands over the money, trusting my knowledge of her tastes and desires, then takes the credit for the presents under the tree at Christmas or for her birthday.

THE GOD FACTOR

God gave the greatest gift. Much more than just a story we read in church around the Christmas holiday, God offered a Savior and a life worth living on earth and the promise of eternity in Heaven with Him. All this at the highest cost ever paid for anything. "For God so loved the world that He gave His one and only Son, that whoever believes in Him shall not perish but have eternal life" (John 3:16). Have you accepted this precious gift?

God has also demonstrated His love for us through the gift of His Word, the Bible. His very words of truth, love, and hope to you and to me, written down by his choice servants and preserved through the ages.

Also think with me of Jesus' gift to us when He left this world to go back to prepare a place in Heaven for us. It was then that Jesus gave us the Holy Spirit who lives in the heart of every believer (John 15:26; 16:5–15).

God has graciously given us everything we need to live the lives to which He calls us. Second Timothy 1:7 says, "For God did not give us a spirit of timidity, but a spirit of power, of love and of self-discipline." Indeed, "every good and perfect gift is from above, coming down from the Father of the heavenly lights, who does not change like shifting shadows" (James 1:17).

And the *way* God gives is significantly different from the world's gift-giving practices. Jesus said to the disciples, "Peace I leave with you; my peace I give you. I do not give to you as the world gives. Do not let your hearts be troubled and do not be afraid" (John 14:27). God graciously provides our every need and more—never taking back, not withholding because we don't deserve His gifts, not waiting until He sees if we give Him a gift, not giving as a bribe. We have much to learn from Him about giving!

Praying **for My Sweetheart**

Thank You for this generous person who enjoys tangible reminders of my love. *Help me remember* that it is the thought and the attitude with which I plan and give to _____ that counts. Help me be creative and generous and regularly give gifts.

A HAPPY ENDING

Jamie waited with a little apprehension for Bryce to come home from work. Would he be mad at her for spending money on the flowers she sent him at work, or did he like them and feel special? She was upstairs in the bedroom when she heard his cheery greeting.

"Hi, Bryce," she called from upstairs, "I'll be down in a minute."

As usual, she found him foraging in the kitchen for a snack. "That will spoil your dinner, and I'm almost ready to put it on the table."

"Hmmm, smells good too." He gave her a longer-than-usual hug.

"Hmmm, this is good too," Jamie said from inside the circle of his arms. "What's up?"

Instead of letting go and moving away, he pulled her closer and rested his chin on top of her head. "I was the envy of my department at work today."

"Oh, yeah? How so?" Jamie held her breath. So far, so good.

"Some really thoughtful woman sent me flowers." He backed away just far enough that he could look into her eyes. "I love you too."

Bryce left the next morning earlier than usual for a meeting. After finishing the breakfast dishes, Jamie went up to their room to make the bed and get ready to go to her job. Under her pillow was her favorite candy bar with a little slip of paper that read, "Gotcha! Feel loved? I do! ~Bryce."

TIME TOGETHER FOR THE TWO OF YOU

1. Consider the following scale, ranging from one (1) "Gifts don't mean that much to me" to five (5) "gifts really make me feel loved." One at a time, share where you'd rank this love language and explain your choice.

2. If you chose a four (4) or five (5) on the scale, tell your partner of the most recent times when you felt loved because of gifts. Then offer other suggestions on ways your partner can express love in this language, or mention some of the fifty-two suggestions below that you find appealing.

If you are reading alone without the interaction of your partner, observe, experiment, or directly ask questions.

Talk Easy Listen Hard

52

WAYS TO USE

Gifts

to EXPRESS
Your Love:

1 Candy
2 Favorite homemade cookies
3 Flowers
4 Clothing or accessories
5 A collectible (what do they like?)
6 A trip or day away
7 Favorite magazine
8 Pay for something you usually don't
9 A homemade craft
10 A little something mailed to the office
11 A favorite snack
12 Favorite food
13 Favorite team clothing or item
14 Book by favorite author
15 CD of favorite music
16 Jewelry
17 A tree planted in their honor
18 A personalized keepsake
19 Photo album with pictures inside
20 Chocolate
21 A soft bath towel
22 Satin or flannel sheets
23 Perfume or cologne
24 Lingerie or silk boxers
25 Ingredients for dinner for two
26 Dinner out

27 A candle
28 A favorite hot or cold drink
29 A bunch of wild flowers
30 A red rose
31 A gift certificate
32 A new wallet with a picture of you in it
33 One of your best photos
34 A cuddly pet
35 Something they have hinted about
36 Two hours of free time
37 A "free" afternoon
38 Money
39 An electric toothbrush
40 Appointment book (add dates with you!)
41 Get a favorite movie
42 An indoor picnic when it rains
43 A certificate for a tool or auto item
44 Tickets to a ball game
45 A restaurant or coffee shop gift card
46 A single flower
47 A beautiful greeting card
48 A handmade note
49 An electronic massager
50 A piece of artwork
51 Something in their favorite color
52 A fun game

Love Language: Loving Gifts

CHAPTER

12

Acts of Service

Because Rich's primary love language is acts of service, I am always looking for little things I can do that tell him by my actions, "I love you!" One snowy day in Pennsylvania, when I knew Rich would be coming home from a trucking stint within a few hours, I looked out the window and realized his car had been parked at the truck lot during the heavy snowfall of the past two days. Delighted to find something I could do to show my love, I put the shovel, broom, and extra set of car keys in the Jeep and four-wheeled over to the lot.

Sure enough his car was parked in a line of cars that were completely covered with almost a foot of slowly melting snow. And the snowplow had done a good job of barricading the whole line with a two-foot wall of snow pushed up against their bumpers.

About an hour later, I'd heated up the car from the inside, brushed off the outside, and shoveled the snow from around the car. I'd even made a path out of the line and onto the cleared lot. Happy with myself and thankful the Lord had given me a fun and visible way to demonstrate my love for Rich, I hopped back in the Jeep and headed home to shovel the driveway.

Pamper Me, Please!

How true is each statement for you?
(5—Definitely to 1—Not particularly)

▶ When I come home late and find dinner
  ready on the table, I'm in heaven! ....5—4—3—2—1

▶ I love being surprised by a freshly washed
  and vacuumed car. ....5—4—3—2—1

▶ I need chicken soup and to be fussed over
  when I'm sick. ....5—4—3—2—1

▶ I love it when my spouse comes out
  and helps me with the yard work. ....5—4—3—2—1

▶ I like the checkout line where they bag
  my groceries for me. ....5—4—3—2—1

▶ I really appreciate if someone offers to
  take a responsibility from me when I'm
  not feeling well. ....5—4—3—2—1

Total your points. A score of 20–30 means you relate strongly to the love language of acts of service.

GOTTA KNOW INFO

Most of us enjoy being pampered and taken care of by the people we love. But if, of all the languages, others doing kind things beyond what's expected makes you feel the most loved and cherished, your love language could be acts of service.

Are *you* high energy, thoughtful, always looking for a way to serve the ones you love? You might be Choleric/Melancholy; both these personalities enjoy doing tasks and focus on accomplishments. You might be Sanguine/Choleric and love to bless people with your high energy and Sanguine sensitivity. Even Melancholy/ Phlegmatics enjoy serving others—behind the scenes. Regardless of personality, the ones who speak this language are doers with sensitivity to the other person's needs.

Good News

The good news about acts of service is the financial cost is generally minimal. But nothing worthwhile is ever *free*. Acts of service require time to observe the need, lots of creative planning, and definitely some elbow grease. Even though the service might be free, the thought and energy you put into the activity reflects your love for the person on the receiving end.

In addition, there are endless possibilities for ways in which you can serve another person. As suggested in the last chapter, sitting down with your partner's best friend to get help with your planning can be an excellent idea. With so many options, you won't run out of ways to say "I love you" in a service project!

Challenging News

One of the problems with using acts of service to show someone your love is the possibility that the service will go unnoticed, unneeded, or unappreciated. How does the person know *you* were the one responsible for the freshly mowed lawn—could it have been your neighbor? Maybe your sweetie didn't realize the car was dirty and doesn't realize you slaved over it in the hot driveway for over an hour! What if your act goes completely unnoticed? What if you shovel and then it snows before your spouse has a chance to notice your efforts? Bummer! At least you have the satisfaction of knowing that you and God know about your demonstration of love.

Another problem with acts of service is these acts can become expected. Nothing takes the joy out of doing something nice more than these two things: an order for you to do it, or it being taken for granted. Earlier in our marriage I remember Rich asking me how I could possibly stand up and speak to thousands of women but could *not* get the wash done on a regular basis.

Let me explain that I interpreted *done* to mean the laundry has made it through the washer and drier and can be worn if you go to the basement and get it yourself. That didn't mean I never folded and put away the laundry. I did when I remembered—but out of sight (down the basement) is out of mind. I'm getting better about leaving notes for myself and setting timers.

Rich's version of *done* means cleaned, dried, folded, ironed, and put away. In his own words, "If it's not in the drawers, it's not done." For a while I resented him for this—until I read Dr. Chapman's book on love languages. And then getting the wash all the way done became a way I could demonstrate my love for Rich. Even though he only compliments me once in a blue moon, I have the satisfaction of knowing I'm loving him in his own special way.

The acts of service love language can be bad news if you're tired. Life can be a rat race with too many things to do in too little time. Let me ask you a question that may have a difficult answer. If your partner's love language is acts of service and you don't have time to do extra little things to show him your love, does he know you love him? When is it enough? When can you stop? Remember that God never asks us or calls us to do more than we are able or more than He will equip us to do. I believe the answer for those of us who are tired comes in two parts. One, with God's help, reevaluate your schedule and priorities. And two, pray for energy and strength, even in the little things. After all, "'til death do us part" is supposed to mean a lifetime of loving each other.

THE GOD FACTOR

Whoever wants to become great among you must be your servant, and whoever wants to be first must be your slave—just as the Son of Man did not come to be served, but to serve, and to give His life as a ransom for many" (Matthew 20:26–28). Acts of service isn't a new concept. God designed humanity to serve each other and to serve and glorify Him. The concept is so important to Him that He sent His Son to exemplify the principle for us.

How does God serve us? Jesus shocked the disciples by washing their feet, customarily a task of one of the least important servants in an establishment. And today God continues to do kind things for us—we call them blessings. When did you last bless the Lord? And how have you blessed your loved one by serving in some delightfully creative and kind way?

> ### Praying for My Sweetheart
>
> *Thank You* for this person of action. Thank You for all that
> _____ does for me. *Help me remember* to accomplish
> tasks without grumbling or complaining—but with the thought,
> "I am choosing to do this for you because I love you."
> Please make me creative and daily show me some small,
> encouraging action I can perform.

A HAPPY ENDING

As I tossed the last shovelful of snow onto the drift-covered lawn, I turned to see Rich's little maroon car pulling into the clean driveway. I thanked the Lord again for good timing and waited to see what Rich would say after he parked at the end of the drive.

Much to my delight, I heard his cheerful voice boom, "Might you know who made sure my car was the only one that wasn't covered with snow and had a tiny little path leading right out to the cleared area?"

I cleared my throat and shot back, "Did it make you feel loved?"

"Sure did." He had almost reached me at the other end of the driveway, and I could see his eyes shining and his big grin.

"Then that would have been me." I sighed with delight as he pulled me into his arms—and we both felt loved!

TIME TOGETHER FOR THE TWO OF YOU

1. Consider the following scale, ranging from one (1) "Acts of service don't mean that much to me" to five (5) "service really makes me feel loved." One at a time, share where you'd rank this love language and explain your choice.

2. If you chose a four (4) or five (5) on the scale, tell your partner of the most recent times when you felt loved because of service. Then offer other suggestions on ways your partner can express love in this language, or mention some of the fifty-two suggestions below that you find appealing.

If you are reading alone without the interaction of your partner, observe, experiment, or directly ask questions.

52

WAYS TO USE

Acts

of Service
to EXPRESS
Your Love:

1 Making a favorite meal for dinner

2 Cleaning up the kitchen or bathroom

3 Planning a scavenger hunt

4 Doing something on their to-do list

5 Getting the newspaper

6 Doing their yard work or chores

7 Going the extra mile

8 Deliver a glass of cold water

9 Baking favorite cookies

10 Picking her up at work on a snowy night

11 Presenting breakfast in bed

12 Fixing something broken

13 Write or type a message dictated to you

14 Washing their automobile

15 Planning a special surprise event

16 Planning a special outing for two

17 Keeping fresh juice or tea in the fridge

18 Helping out with a responsibility

19 Giving him a massage

20 Giving her a manicure/pedicure

21 Doing the annual tax preparation

22 Mowing the lawn

23 Making appointments for them

24 Warming the dinner plates or coffee cups

25 Making an extra special breakfast

26 Record a favorite TV show or sports event

27 Balancing the checkbook

28 Picking out a special outfit

29 Cleaning up after kids or pets

30 Getting the mail

31 Getting a hot drink on a cold day

32 Getting a cold drink on a hot day

33 Running errands for them

34 Keeping up with household duties

35 Making the bed

36 Good manners like holding the door

37 Carrying in the groceries

38 Washing the dishes

39 Helping reorganize a personal space

40 Doing the laundry

41 Taking out the garbage

42 Washing the windows

43 Putting up or taking down decorations

44 Shoveling the driveway or sidewalk

45 Going to parents' night at school

46 Helping with a PTA project

47 Volunteering to help a favorite charity

48 Going to the store for groceries

49 Renting or returning a movie

50 Helping with a project for work

51 Care when they are ill

52 Putting on or picking up coffee

13

QuaLity TiMe
WiTH tHe
ONe YoU Love

Emily looked at Bill through her tears. "I just . . . *sniff* . . . need to know . . . *sniff* . . . if you still . . . *sniff, pause, sniff* . . . love me." She hiccupped and covered her face with her hands.

Bill was bewildered. He dropped his briefcase and walked over to Emily, gently pulling her down to the couch and sitting beside her. "Baby, what do you mean? Where is this coming from?" He smoothed her hair and tried to wipe her tears away, but she was hiding her face from him. "I tell you I love you all the time, honey. I bring you flowers and buy you beautiful things."

Emily's sobs just got louder.

"I do all the yard work myself and get you a housekeeper to clean once a week." His eyes opened wide, and taking hold of her chin with gentle firmness, he lifted her head so he could see her face. "I'm not interested in another soul. You're the only one for me, ever." His voice, which rang with sincerity, broke on that last word. He hugged her to himself and whispered, "I love you, Em."

Hugging him back for all she was worth, Emily whispered fiercely, "Don't let me go. I was so afraid." She hiccupped again, and Bill rubbed her back soothingly. In a tiny, quivery voice, she said, "You never spend any time with me anymore."

Bill gradually pulled away until he could look into Emily's face. "I need to work, honey, so I can give you what you need."

"But Bill, I don't want stuff. I want you! I'd gladly go back to our smaller house and work my old part-time job if we could spend our evenings together again and spontaneously pack the kids off to the grandparents for a weekend so we can stay in bed and . . . well, you know." With pink cheeks and downcast eyes, Emily fiddled with a button on Bill's shirt.

Bill took a deep breath and leaned back on the couch, pulling Emily along with him. Cradling her in his arms, he tried to remember the last time they'd sat on this couch together or even held each other for this long—outside of their bedroom. "I'm sorry, Em. You're right. I don't know how this happened."

Emily lay in his arms and silently communicated with God. *Oh, thank you, Lord, for helping him see. Please help him do something about it. Give me patience, Lord.* Suddenly Emily realized Bill had grown very quiet. "Thank you, honey." She snuggled closer into his arms.

"For what, baby?"

"For holding me tonight and talking to me and explaining how you love me. I think sometimes we speak in different languages when it comes to love."

Time Out

How true is each statement for you?
(5—Definitely to 1—Not particularly)

▶ I love Christmas when we get to spend
the whole day together with family. ....5—4—3—2—1

Talk Easy Listen Hard

▶ I don't need fancy gifts and services—I just
  want my sweetheart to hang out with me. ....5—4—3—2—1

▶ I really enjoy getting snowed in together
  for a day or two. ....5—4—3—2—1

▶ I would feel incredibly special if my spouse
  took a day off work to be with me. ....5—4—3—2—1

▶ I like sitting together, watching the sunset,
  and talking about our dreams. ....5—4—3—2—1

▶ I feel so encouraged when we work together. ....5—4—3—2—1

*A score of 20–30 means you relate strongly to the love language
of quality time.*

GOTTA KNOW INFO

Spending quality time with someone demonstrates the intangible quality of love. It says you care enough to share your most precious commodity—time. Some people who speak this language want one-on-one focused you-and-me time. Others more simply just want to be with you—it doesn't matter if you are both doing different activities, as long as you are in the same room or within speaking distance. There is a delightful reassurance in the presence of another human being, especially one we love.

Looking at the personalities, it is not hard to come up with the Phlegmatic as the one who speaks the love language of time. These gentle, laid-back individuals love being surrounded by their favorite people. Both Sanguines and Phlegmatics are relationship oriented and focused on people. But the Sanguine flits from flower to flower, never able to settle down for long periods of time with their profound energy level. That leaves the peaceful, relaxed Phlegmatic most often hanging out with loved ones.

Good News

One benefit of spending time together is the negligible financial cost. You don't need to take an expensive and exotic cruise together in order to spend quality time, although that might be fun. Most often spending time together is a simple gift that takes little money.

Quality time can happen anywhere. Think of it as stopping the world and getting off for a little while—whenever you can, wherever you are, and for however long you can afford. You focus on each other and spend the time in activities that draw you together and allow you to communicate your love and commitment to each other.

Challenging News

This is a need that can easily be overlooked. My husband and I share the Choleric personality—he is a Choleric/Melancholy and I'm a Sanguine/Choleric. Neither one of us possesses Phlegmatic tendencies, therefore we spend little time hanging out together without being active and purpose driven. If, however, I was married to a person with Phlegmatic tendencies, I might easily overlook his need for quality time together. I could energetically take care of him, create a lovely home, and plan fun things for us to do together, but I might overlook his very real need to just hang out and talk.

The other tricky aspect of this love language is figuring out *how* to spend this time together. Do you have a Sanguine loved one who wants to do activities *with you*? Or is your sweetheart more Phlegmatic and low-key and just needs you to devote a few evenings a week to hanging out in the family room with him while he watches television and you catch up on chores?

THE GOD FACTOR

God loves you and demonstrates His love in many wonderful ways. In fact, the love languages originated with Him because He *is* love. Of all the languages, quality time is the one that awes me the most. The God of the universe wants to spend time with me.

God wants to spend time with *you*! Just read Psalm 139 to get a picture of how God knows you and loves you. And He said, "Never will I leave you; never will I forsake you" (Hebrews 13:5; and see Deuteronomy 31:6). "Surely I am with you always, to the very end of the age" (Matthew 28:20). And God's not just about quantity,

M

Talk Easy Listen Hard

He's quality through and through. When He says He's here for you that means He is actively working all things together for your good and His glory—always.

A HAPPY ENDING

That next Friday evening, Bill came home early from work with several bags in his arms and a secretive expression on his face.

"Hey, mister, what are you up to?" Emily was back to her normal sunny self. She made a halfhearted effort to look into one of the bags and Bill whisked her away.

"Okay, here's the deal. You pack up Timmy and the baby for a two-day stay at your folks . . ."

"What?" Emily's expression was priceless.

"And then I'll run them over to Mom and Dad's while you get dressed to go out for dinner. You should have about thirty-five, forty minutes. Any questions?" He put up his hand, looking rather pleased with himself. "On second thought, no questions allowed." He grinned. "This weekend you're stuck with me for two whole days. You asked for it, you know!"

Emily twirled around like a little girl and then rushed at Bill and kissed him soundly on the cheek before hurrying off to get the kids ready to go. She couldn't wait!

AN IMPORTANT REMINDER

Real-life relationships don't always have a happy ending like you found at the conclusion of each of the love languages chapters.

m

But God has promised us a joyful union with the Prince of Peace (Isaiah 9:6 and Acts 5:31) who will come again someday riding on a white horse (Revelation 19:6–11). It is going to be so spectacular the Bible compares it to a wedding feast and marriage—but unlike relationships on earth, it will be completely perfect. When this short life is over, believers will spend eternity in God's presence, and this life with its temporary troubles will seem like the blink of an eye.

If you and your partner don't have similar personalities, if you don't think the same, and if your love languages seem worlds apart, know first and foremost that there is One who completely knows and perfectly loves you. He will meet your needs, even if your sweetheart doesn't, can't, or won't. And as He meets your needs, He will equip you to meet the needs of your partner.

TIME TOGETHER FOR THE TWO OF YOU

1. Consider the following scale, ranging from one (1) "I don't need to be with my partner that much to feel loved" to five (5) "spending quality time together is the best way to feed our relationship." One at a time, share where you'd rank this love language and explain your choice.

2. If you chose a four (4) or five (5) on the scale, tell your partner of the most recent times when you felt loved because of quality time together. Then offer other suggestions on ways your partner can express love in this language, or mention some of the fifty-two suggestions below that you find appealing.

If you are reading alone without the interaction of your partner, observe, experiment, or directly ask questions.

Talk Easy Listen Hard

52

WAYS TO USE

Time
Together
to EXPRESS
Your Love:

1 Going out to dinner

2 Going on a leisurely walk through the woods

3 Spending the evening together at home

4 Getting away for the weekend

5 Taking a class together

6 Working on a project together

7 Participating together in sports

8 Going sightseeing

9 Playing games

10 Just hanging out and talking

11 Lunch at a favorite restaurant

12 Breakfast out

13 Breakfast in bed—together

14 Accompanying him to a sports event

15 Accompanying her to a concert

16 Going on a picnic together

17 Playing hide-and-seek

18 A walk in the moonlight

19 A walk on the beach

20 Participating in a favorite activity

21 Starting a new hobby together

22 Creating something artistic together

23 Visiting the library

24 Reading aloud a book you will both enjoy

25 Window-shopping downtown

26 Going grocery shopping

27 Going out for coffee

28 Sleeping in

29 Cooking together

30 Baking together

31 Making candy or snacks

32 Taking a drive in the countryside

33 Walking around a major city

34 Visiting a museum

35 Going to garage sales and bargain hunting

36 Poking around a bookstore

37 Visiting an older relative

38 Playing in an arcade

39 Going to an amusement park

40 Planning a party together

41 Running errands together

42 Taking a nap in the middle of the day

43 Going to church together

44 Watching a television program or movie

45 Going on vacation

46 Driving around to see Christmas lights

47 Double-dating with friends

48 Spending time with extended family

49 Going for a boat ride

50 Studying together

51 Doing a home-repair job together

52 Working on the lawn and gardens

Love Language: Quality Time

Test Your Learning and Your Memory!

1. A Personality is:
   a) a funny guy on the late show
   b) the internal wiring that motivates a person's words
      and actions

2. A Thought Continuum is:
   a) a meeting of philosophers and other wise thinkers
   b) the extremes of our thought processes

3. A Love Language is:
   a) one of the languages spoken on a tropical island
   b) one of five unique ways we express love and by
      which we feel loved

If you answered *b* every time, you get an A+! Okay, that was easy. But, seriously, what's next? Now that you know so much more about yourself and your partner, communication should be a breeze, right?

Wrong. Conversation will *always* take thought, because words come from the brain. With the exception of God, you must work at understanding others and speaking their languages. Even though you may study and know yourself and your partner very, very well, there will be times when you still think differently—and that's good!

Some may ask, "But what if we're just *too* different?" Society tells us it's okay to scrap a marriage if it doesn't turn out the way we expected. Take a good look at who God is. He never quits, never gives up, and always comes through for us when we need Him. He is the Master of reconciliation—He proved it on the cross! By His grace, the two of you can make a go of your relationship if you do it God's way.

I believed God designed us in such a way that communication will always, this side of heaven, be challenging. But challenge keeps us on our toes. It pushes us beyond mediocrity to a continual state of learning and depending on God, who knows it all.

So where do we go from here?

Okay, Now What?

1. *Relax!* One of the most awesome effects this material has on the learner is a feeling of relief. Maybe for the first time in your life you realize it's okay to not be good at everything. God perfectly creates us with holes so that we desperately need Him, and on an earthly level we need other people in the world around us. While we teach ourselves to compensate for areas of weakness, when stress, fatigue, sickness, and tragedy strike, and when the things we have added to our innate inner wiring fall away, we're back at square one. Do you understand the real you a bit better? Hallelujah to the God who perfectly and sovereignly created us, knows, and loves us. How important it is for us to keep up a personal relationship with Him every day of our lives. So take a moment to smile and praise God for who you are and what He is doing in your life—and keep the relationship going.

2. *Capitalize on Strengths.* From the information you learned about yourself, use your strengths to better your relationship with your loved one and serve the Lord! He uniquely formed you to do the things He's prepared in advance for you to do (Ephesians 2:10).

3. *Compensate for Weaknesses.* Because Rich and I have studied personality for many years, it was natural for us to wonder about our daughter's personality when she arrived on the scene. We didn't realize how much she was picking up until, at about age six, she proclaimed, "I don't have to remember that—I'm Sanguine." Oh, no, no, no! Just because you may have a weakness, don't use it as an excuse. You may always have a particular bad tendency, but as a Christian you have the Overcomer living within you (1 John 5:3–5). While you won't always do the right thing, God can help you in your weakness (Romans 8:26). In fact, *His* strength shows up best in our weaknesses (2 Corinthians 12:9–10).

4. *Forgive and Release Your Partner's Weaknesses.* One of the most lovely benefits of studying this material is finding out your partner isn't annoying you on purpose—they are just wired that way! But since you can't change the weaknesses of the other person, you are faced with a choice. You can focus on their sin, selfishness, and weaknesses, allowing these things to get the best of both of

Talk Easy Listen Hard

you. Or you can follow God's example and be forgiving, even when the other person hasn't asked and when they don't deserve it. That's what we were like when Jesus died for our sins. Coming to the relationship with a spirit of forgiveness and understanding, you will truly be able to see clearly and communicate effectively. If you hold on to resentment, anger, and pride, your clouded vision will make it impossible to focus. Choose grace!

5. *Encourage Your Partner.* Scripture tells us in no uncertain terms we must learn to be positive and encouraging towards each other—always ready to think the best. Yes, once in a while we must deal with an area of sin, weakness, or conflict, but then *get back to being positive.* Check out the truths in Philippians 2:1–4; 4:4, 8; and Hebrews 3:13; 10:22–25. One of the most effective ways I keep myself positive about Rich is by focusing on a small piece of paper I keep in the back of my Bible on which I list his strengths and things I love about him. When I get frustrated and tempted to take back an area of weakness I've committed to God for safekeeping, I pull out the list and refresh my mind (Romans 12:2).

6. *Communicate Smarter.* Now you've got tools to make communicating easier. I'm praying that you will be a more attentive listener and that you will be able to resolve (and maybe even prevent) conflicts more effectively. Then your respect and credibility will increase so much that your partner will want to listen to what you have to say because you know how to speak their language.

The Creator awaits to take you from here. "The Lord gives wisdom, and from His mouth come knowledge and understanding" (Proverbs 2:6). He is indeed able to do "immeasurably more than all we ask or imagine, according to His power that is at work within us" for our good and His glory (Ephesians 3:20). May we apply what we have learned so that "speaking the truth in love, we will in all things grow up into Him who is the Head, that is Christ. From Him the whole body, joined and held together by every supporting ligament, grows and builds itself up in love, as each part does its work" (Ephesians 4:15–16). May it be so.

Loving Creator and Perfect Communicator,
Thank You for designing us with differences.
We need You to continue this journey with us
to teach us how to value and use our new understanding
*   of each other.*
Help us shed our self-centered actions and reactions.
and focus our attention, love, and understanding on each other.
Make us wise, forgiving, and unconditionally loving—as You are.
Teach us to unite our hearts and minds
so we can demonstrate to the world a godly example
*   of true reconciliation,*
a godly marriage of two very different people
who are learning to really communicate!
We give You the praise, O God! Amen.

APPENDIX A

PERSONAL PROFILES

His Profile . . . How He's Motivated:

SANGUINE	CHOLERIC
+ popular	+ powerful
+ talkative	+ concise
+ dramatic	+ a strong leader
+ optimistic	+ realistic
+ a people-pleaser	+ results oriented
- forgetful	- arrogant
- lacks follow-thru	- controlling
- a poor listener	- brusque
Basic Desire: **FUN**	*Basic Desire:* **CONTROL**
PHLEGMATIC	**MELANCHOLY**
+ peaceful	+ perfect
+ a good listener	+ analytical
+ loyal	+ sensitive
+ relaxed	+ conscientious
+ a people-lover	+ task oriented
- a procrastinator	- critical
- nonconfrontational	- moody
- tuned out	- withdrawn
Basic Desire: **PEACE**	*Basic Desire:* **PERFECTION**

Using the chart above or your results from appendix B, write next to the personality types the percentages of each you see in the male partner.

Sanguine _____%   Melancholy _____%

Choleric _____%   Phlegmatic _____%

Describe his strengths: _____

_____

_____

_____

_____

_____

_____

_____

_____

_____

_____

_____

_____

How He Thinks:

Circle a dot on each continuum where he fits between these opposite traits.

Internal . . . . External

Concrete . . . . Abstract

Sequential . . . . .Random

Global. . . . . Analytical

How He Loves:

Number the following love languages in his preferred order (1-highest, 5-lowest).

_____ **Words** He needs to hear/gives words of affirmation, love, and encouragement

_____ **Gifts** He enjoys giving/getting gifts & cards—tangible expressions

_____ **Acts** He serves you and/or appreciates it when you do things for him.

_____ **Touch** He needs/gives affectionate touches, strokes, hugs, and massages

_____ **Time** He wants to spend special times or just ordinary times *together*

SANGUINE	CHOLERIC
+ popular	+ powerful
+ talkative	+ concise
+ dramatic	+ a strong leader
+ optimistic	+ realistic
+ a people-pleaser	+ results oriented
- forgetful	- arrogant
- lacks follow-thru	- controlling
- a poor listener	- brusque
Basic Desire: **FUN**	*Basic Desire:* **CONTROL**
PHLEGMATIC	**MELANCHOLY**
+ peaceful	+ perfect
+ a good listener	+ analytical
+ loyal	+ sensitive
+ relaxed	+ conscientious
+ a people-lover	+ task oriented
- a procrastinator	- critical
- nonconfrontational	- moody
- tuned out	- withdrawn
Basic Desire: **PEACE**	*Basic Desire:* **PERFECTION**

Using the chart above or your results from appendix B, write next to the personality types the percentages of each you see in the female partner.

Sanguine _____%   Melancholy _____%

Choleric _____%   Phlegmatic _____%

Describe her strengths: _____

_____

_____

_____

_____

_____

_____

_____

_____

_____

_____

_____

_____

How She Thinks:

Circle a dot on each continuum where she fits between these opposite traits.

Internal . . . . External

Concrete . . . . Abstract

Sequential . . . . .Random

Global. . . . . Analytical

How She Loves:

Number the following love languages in her preferred order (1-highest, 5-lowest).

_____ **Words** She needs to hear/gives words of affirmation, love, and encouragement

_____ **Gifts** She enjoys giving/getting gifts & cards—tangible expressions

_____ **Acts** She serves you and/or appreciates it when you do things for her.

_____ **Touch** She needs/gives affectionate touches, strokes, hugs, and massages

_____ **Time** She wants to spend special times or just ordinary times _together_

Personal Profiles

PErSONALity
QueStiONNaire

DIRECTIONS:

For each group of four words, put an X in the box beside the word that **most** often applies to you. If you have difficulty choosing a word, ask your spouse or a friend, and think of how you were as a child—going back to your natural personality. Caution: do not take too long to ponder your answer; go with your initial reaction. At the end of the forty sets of words, you will find additional directions. (Definitions adapted from Personality Patterns by Lana Bateman)

STRENGTHS

1 ☐ **Adventurous** — *One who will take on new and daring challenges with a determination to master them*

☐ **Adaptable** — *Easily fits and is comfortable in any situation*

☐ **Animated** — *Full of life, lively use of hand, arm, and face gestures*

☐ **Analytical** — *Likes to examine the parts for their logical and proper relationships*

2 ☐ **Persistent** — *Sees one project through to its completion before starting another*

☐ **Playful** — *Full of fun and good humor*

☐ **Persuasive** — *Convinces through logic and fact rather than charm or power*

☐ **Peaceful** — *Seems undisturbed and tranquil and retreats from any form of strife*

3 ☐ **Submissive** — *Easily accepts any other's point of view or desire with little need to assert his opinion*

☐ **Self-sacrificing** — *Willingly gives up his own personal being for the sake of, or to meet the needs of, others*

☐ **Sociable** — *One who sees being with others as an opportunity to be entertaining rather than as a challenge or business opportunity*

☐ **Strong willed** — *Determined to have one's own way*

4 ☐ **Considerate**   *Having regard for the needs and feelings of others*

☐ **Controlled**   *Has emotional feelings but rarely displays them*

☐ **Competitive**   *Turns every situation, happening, or game into a contest and always plays to win!*

☐ **Convincing**   *Can win you over to anything through the sheer charm of his personality*

5 ☐ **Refreshing**   *Renews and stimulates or makes others feel good*

☐ **Respectful**   *Treats others with deference, honor, and esteem*

☐ **Reserved**   *Self-restrained in expression of emotion or enthusiasm*

☐ **Resourceful**   *Able to act quickly and effectively in virtually all situations*

6 ☐ **Satisfied**   *A person who easily accepts any circumstance or situation*

☐ **Sensitive**   *Intensively cares about others and what happens*

☐ **Self-reliant**   *An independent person who can fully rely on own capabilities, judgment, and resources*

☐ **Spirited**   *Full of life and excitement*

7 ☐ **Planner**   *Prefers to work out a detailed arrangement beforehand, for the accomplishment of project or goal, and prefers involvement with the planning stages and the finished product rather than the carrying out of the task*

☐ **Patient**   *Unmoved by delay, remains calm and tolerant*

☐ **Positive**   *Knows it will turn out right if he's in charge*

☐ **Promoter**   *Urges or compels others to go along, join, or invest through the charm of his own personality*

8 ☐ **Sure**   *Confident, rarely hesitates or wavers*

☐ **Spontaneous**   *Prefers all of life to be impulsive, unpremeditated activity, not restricted by plans*

☐ **Scheduled**   *Makes, and lives, according to a daily plan, dislikes his plan to be interrupted*

☐ **Shy**   *Quiet, doesn't easily instigate a conversation*

    Talk Easy Listen Hard

9 ☐ **Orderly** — *Having a methodical, systematic arrangement of things*

☐ **Obliging** — *Accommodating; one who is quick to do it another's way*

☐ **Outspoken** — *Speaks frankly and without reserve*

☐ **Optimistic** — *Sunny disposition who convinces self and others that everything will turn out all right*

10 ☐ **Friendly** — *A responder rather than an initiator, seldom starts a conversation*

☐ **Faithful** — *Consistently reliable, steadfast, loyal, and devoted sometimes beyond reason*

☐ **Funny** — *Sparkling sense of humor that can make virtually any story into an hilarious event*

☐ **Forceful** — *A commanding personality whom others would hesitate to take a stand against*

11 ☐ **Daring** — *Willing to take risks; fearless, bold*

☐ **Delightful** — *A person who is upbeat and fun to be with*

☐ **Diplomatic** — *Deals with people tactfully, sensitively, and patiently*

☐ **Detailed** — *Does everything in proper order with a clear memory of all the things that happen*

12 ☐ **Cheerful** — *Consistently in good spirits and promoting happiness in others*

☐ **Consistent** — *Stays emotionally on an even keel, responding as one might expect*

☐ **Cultured** — *One whose interests involve both intellectual and artistic pursuits, such as theater, symphony, ballet*

☐ **Confident** — *Self-assured and certain of own ability and success*

13 ☐ **Idealistic** *Visualizes things in their perfect form, and has a need to measure up to that standard himself*

☐ **Independent** *Self-sufficient, self-supporting, self-confident, and seems to have little need of help*

☐ **Inoffensive** *A person who never says or causes anything unpleasant or objectionable*

☐ **Inspiring** *Encourages others to work, join, or be involved, and makes the whole thing fun*

14 ☐ **Demonstrative** *Openly expresses emotion, especially affection, and doesn't hesitate to touch others while speaking to them*

☐ **Decisive** *A person with quick, conclusive, judgment-making ability*

☐ **Dry humor** *Exhibits dry wit, usually one-liners which can be sarcastic in nature*

☐ **Deep** *Intense and often introspective with a distaste for surface conversation and pursuits*

15 ☐ **Mediator** *Consistently finds himself in the role of reconciling differences in order to avoid conflict*

☐ **Musical** *Participates in or has a deep appreciation for music, committed to music as an art form rather than the fun of performance*

☐ **Mover** *Driven by a need to be productive, is a leader whom others follow, finds it difficult to sit still*

☐ **Mixes Easily** *Loves a party and can't wait to meet everyone in the room, never meets a stranger*

16 ☐ **Thoughtful** *A considerate person who remembers special occasions and is quick to make a kind gesture*

☐ **Tenacious** *Holds on firmly, stubbornly, and won't let go until the goal is accomplished*

☐ **Talker** *Constantly talking, generally telling funny stories and entertaining everyone around, feeling the need to fill the silence in order to make others comfortable*

☐ **Tolerant** *Easily accepts the thought and ways of others without the need to disagree with or change them*

Talk Easy Listen Hard

17 ☐	Listener	*Always seems willing to hear what others have to say*
	☐ Loyal	*Faithful to a person, ideal, or job, sometime beyond reason*
	☐ Leader	*A natural-born director, who is driven to be in charge, and often finds it difficult to believe that anyone else can do the job as well*
	☐ Lively	*Full of life, vigorous, energetic*
18 ☐	Contented	*Easily satisfied with what one has; rarely envious*
	☐ Chief	*Commands leadership and expects people to follow*
	☐ Chartmaker	*Organizes life, tasks, and problem solving by making lists, forms, or graphs*
	☐ Contagious	*Attractive, adorable, center of attention*
19 ☐	Perfectionist	*Places high standards on oneself, and often on others, desiring that everything be in proper order at all times*
	☐ Pleasant	*Easygoing, easy to be around, easy to talk with*
	☐ Productive	*Must constantly be working or achieving, often finds it very difficult to rest*
	☐ Popular	*Life of the party and therefore much desired as a party guest*
20 ☐	Bouncy	*A lively personality, full of energy*
	☐ Bold	*Fearless, daring, forward, unafraid of risk*
	☐ Behaved	*Consistently desires to conduct oneself within the realm of what one feels is proper*
	☐ Balanced	*Stable, middle-of-the-road personality, not subject to sharp highs or lows*

WEAKNESSES

21 ☐	Blank	*A person who shows little facial expression or emotion*
	☐ Bashful	*Shrinks from getting attention, resulting from self-consciousness*
	☐ Brassy	*Showy, flashy, comes on strong, too loud*
	☐ Bossy	*Commanding, domineering, sometimes overbearing in adult relationships*

Personality Questionnaire   197

22 ☐ **Undisciplined** — *A person whose lack of order permeates most every area of his life*

☐ **Unsympathetic** — *Finds it difficult to relate to the problems or hurts of others*

☐ **Unenthusiastic** — *Tends not to get excited, often feeling it won't work anyway*

☐ **Unforgiving** — *One who has difficulty forgiving or forgetting a hurt or injustice done to them, apt to hold onto a grudge*

23 ☐ **Reticent** — *Unwilling or struggles against getting involved, especially when complex*

☐ **Resentful** — *Often holds ill feelings as a result of real or imagined offenses*

☐ **Resistant** — *Strives, works against, or hesitates to accept any other way but his own*

☐ **Repetitious** — *Retells stories and incidents to entertain others without realizing they have already told the story several times before; is constantly needing to say something*

24 ☐ **Fussy** — *Insistent over petty matters or details, calling for a great attention to trivial details*

☐ **Fearful** — *Often experiences feelings of deep concern, apprehension, or anxiousness*

☐ **Forgetful** — *Lack of memory which is usually tied to a lack of discipline and not bothering to mentally record things that aren't fun*

☐ **Frank** — *Straightforward, outspoken, and doesn't mind telling others exactly what they think*

25 ☐ **Impatient** — *A person who finds it difficult to endure irritation or wait for others*

☐ **Insecure** — *One who is apprehensive or lacks confidence*

☐ **Indecisive** — *A person who finds it difficult to make any decision at all (not a personality who labors long over each decision in order to make the perfect one)*

☐ **Interrupts** — *A person who is more of a talker than a listener, who starts speaking without even realizing someone else is already speaking*

    Talk Easy Listen Hard

26 ☐ **Unpopular** — *A person whose intensity and demand for perfection can push others away*

☐ **Uninvolved** — *Has no desire to listen or become interested in clubs, groups, activities, or other people's lives*

☐ **Unpredictable** — *May be ecstatic one moment and down the next, or willing to help but then disappears, or promises to come but forgets to show up*

☐ **Unaffectionate** — *Finds it difficult to verbally or physically demonstrate tenderness openly*

27 ☐ **Headstrong** — *Insists on having their own way*

☐ **Haphazard** — *Has no consistent way of doing things*

☐ **Hard to please** — *A person whose standards are set so high that it is difficult to ever satisfy them*

☐ **Hesitant** — *Slow to get moving and hard to get involved*

28 ☐ **Plain** — *Personality without great highs or lows and showing little, if any, emotion*

☐ **Pessimistic** — *While hoping for the best, this person generally sees the downside of a situation first*

☐ **Proud** — *One with great self-esteem who sees himself as always right and the best person for the job*

☐ **Permissive** — *Allows others (including children) to do as they please in order to keep from being disliked*

29 ☐ **Angered easily** — *One who has a childlike flash-in-the-pan temper that expresses itself in tantrum style and is over and forgotten almost instantly*

☐ **Aimless** — *Not a goal-setter with little desire to be one*

☐ **Argumentative** — *Incites arguments generally because they are right no matter what the situation may be*

☐ **Alienated** — *Easily feels estranged from others, often because of insecurity or fear that others don't really enjoy their company*

30 ☐ **Naïve**   *Simple and childlike perspective, lacking sophistication or comprehension of what the deeper levels of life are really about*

☐ **Negative attitude** *One whose attitude is seldom positive and is often able to see only the down, or dark, side of each situation*

☐ **Nervy**   *Full of confidence, fortitude, and sheer guts, often in a negative sense*

☐ **Nonchalant**   *Easygoing, unconcerned, indifferent*

31 ☐ **Worrier**   *Consistently feels uncertain, troubled, or anxious*

☐ **Withdrawn**   *A person who pulls back within oneself and needs a great deal of alone, or isolation, time*

☐ **Workaholic**   *An aggressive goal-setter who must be constantly productive and feels very guilty when resting, is not driven by a need for perfection or completion but by a need for accomplishment and reward*

☐ **Wants credit**   *Thrives on the credit or approval of others; as an entertainer this person feeds on the applause, laughter, and/or acceptance of an audience*

32 ☐ **Too sensitive**   *Overly introspective and easily offended when misunderstood*

☐ **Tactless**   *Sometimes expresses himself in a somewhat offensive and inconsiderate way*

☐ **Timid**   *Shrinks from difficult situations*

☐ **Talkative**   *An entertaining, compulsive talker who finds it difficult to listen*

33 ☐ **Doubtful**   *Characterized by uncertainty and lack of confidence that it will ever work out*

☐ **Disorganized**   *Lack of ability to ever get life in order*

☐ **Domineering**   *Compulsively takes control of situations and/or people, usually telling others what to do*

☐ **Depressed**   *A person who feels down much of the time*

    Talk Easy Listen Hard

34 ☐ **Inconsistent** *Erratic, contradictory, with actions and emotions not based on logic*

☐ **Introvert** *A person whose thoughts and interests are directed inward; lives within oneself*

☐ **Intolerant** *Appears unable to withstand or accept another's attitudes, point of view, or way of doing things*

☐ **Indifferent** *A person to whom most things don't matter one way or the other*

35 ☐ **Messy** *Living in a state of disorder; unable to find things*

☐ **Moody** *Doesn't get very high emotionally, but easily slips into low lows, often when feeling unappreciated*

☐ **Mumbles** *Will talk quietly under their breath when pushed, doesn't bother to speak clearly*

☐ **Manipulative** *Influences or manages shrewdly or deviously for their own advantage; will get their way somehow*

36 ☐ **Slow** *Doesn't often act or think quickly, too much of a bother*

☐ **Stubborn** *Determined to exert their own will; not easily persuaded; obstinate*

☐ **Show-off** *Needs to be the center of attention, wants to be watched*

☐ **Skeptical** *Disbelieving, questioning the motive behind the words*

37 ☐ **Loner** *Requires a lot of private time and tends to avoid other people*

☐ **Lord over others** *Doesn't hesitate to let others know that they are right or in control*

☐ **Lazy** *Evaluates work or activity in terms of how much energy it will take*

☐ **Loud** *A person whose laugh or voice can be heard above others in the room*

Personality Questionnaire

38 ☐ **Sluggish**   *Slow to get started; needs push to be motivated*

☐ **Suspicious**   *Tends to suspect or distrust others or ideas*

☐ **Short-tempered**   *Has a demanding, impatience-based anger and a short fuse; anger is expressed when others are not moving fast enough or have not completed what they have been asked to do*

☐ **Scatterbrained**   *Lacks the power of concentration or attention; flighty*

39 ☐ **Revengeful**   *Knowingly or otherwise holds a grudge and punishes the offender, often by subtly withholding friendship or affection*

☐ **Restless**   *Likes constant new activity because it isn't fun to do the same things all the time*

☐ **Reluctant**   *Unwilling or struggles against getting involved*

☐ **Rash**   *May act hastily, without thinking things through, generally because of impatience*

40 ☐ **Compromising**   *Will often relax their position, even when right, in order to avoid conflict*

☐ **Critical**   *Constantly evaluating and making judgments, frequently thinking or expressing negative reactions*

☐ **Crafty**   *Shrewd; one who can always find a way to get to the desired end*

☐ **Changeable**   *A childlike, short attention span that needs a lot of change and variety to keep from getting bored*

Further Directions:

Now transfer all your X's to the corresponding words on the following scoring sheet. For example, if you checked *Animated* for number one, check it on the scoring sheet. (Note: the words will be in a different order.) When you have transferred all of your X's, subtotal and total the columns. The *Combined Totals* column with the highest total indicates your primary personality; the next highest score shows your secondary personality. If you multiply each column's combined total by 2.5,

     Talk Easy Listen Hard

you will come up with the percentage of that personality style that fits you. You can place these percentages on your profile in appendix A.

SCORING STRENGTHS

	Popular Sanguine	Powerful Choleric	Perfect Melancholy	Peaceful Phlegmatic
1	☐ Animated	☐ Adventurous	☐ Analytical	☐ Adaptable
2	☐ Playful	☐ Persuasive	☐ Persistent	☐ Peaceful
3	☐ Sociable	☐ Strong willed	☐ Self-sacrificing	☐ Submissive
4	☐ Convincing	☐ Competitive	☐ Considerate	☐ Controlled
5	☐ Refreshing	☐ Resourceful	☐ Respectful	☐ Reserved
6	☐ Spirited	☐ Self-reliant	☐ Sensitive	☐ Satisfied
7	☐ Promoter	☐ Positive	☐ Planner	☐ Patient
8	☐ Spontaneous	☐ Sure	☐ Scheduled	☐ Shy
9	☐ Optimistic	☐ Outspoken	☐ Orderly	☐ Obliging
10	☐ Funny	☐ Forceful	☐ Faithful	☐ Friendly
11	☐ Delightful	☐ Daring	☐ Detailed	☐ Diplomatic
12	☐ Cheerful	☐ Confident	☐ Cultured	☐ Consistent
13	☐ Inspiring	☐ Independent	☐ Idealistic	☐ Inoffensive
14	☐ Demonstrative	☐ Decisive	☐ Deep	☐ Dry humor
15	☐ Mixes Easily	☐ Mover	☐ Musical	☐ Mediator
16	☐ Talker	☐ Tenacious	☐ Thoughtful	☐ Tolerant
17	☐ Lively	☐ Leader	☐ Loyal	☐ Listener
18	☐ Contagious	☐ Chief	☐ Chartmaker	☐ Contented
19	☐ Popular	☐ Productive	☐ Perfectionist	☐ Pleasant
20	☐ Bouncy	☐ Bold	☐ Behaved	☐ Balanced

_____   _____   _____   _____

SUBTOTAL: STRENGTHS

SCORING WEAKNESSES

	Popular Sanguine	Powerful Choleric	Perfect Melancholy	Peaceful Phlegmatic
21	☐ Brassy	☐ Bossy	☐ Bashful	☐ Blank
22	☐ Undisciplined	☐ Unsympathetic	☐ Unforgiving	☐ Unenthusiastic
23	☐ Repetitious	☐ Resistant	☐ Resentful	☐ Reticent
24	☐ Forgetful	☐ Frank	☐ Fussy	☐ Fearful
25	☐ Interrupts	☐ Impatient	☐ Insecure	☐ Indecisive
26	☐ Unpredictable	☐ Unaffectionate	☐ Unpopular	☐ Uninvolved
27	☐ Haphazard	☐ Headstrong	☐ Hard to please	☐ Hesitant
28	☐ Permissive	☐ Proud	☐ Pessimistic	☐ Plain
29	☐ Angered easily	☐ Argumentative	☐ Alienated	☐ Aimless
30	☐ Naïve	☐ Nervy	☐ Negative attitude	☐ Nonchalant
31	☐ Wants credit	☐ Workaholic	☐ Withdrawn	☐ Worrier
32	☐ Talkative	☐ Tactless	☐ Too sensitive	☐ Timid
33	☐ Disorganized	☐ Domineering	☐ Depressed	☐ Doubtful
34	☐ Inconsistent	☐ Intolerant	☐ Introvert	☐ Indifferent
35	☐ Messy	☐ Manipulative	☐ Moody	☐ Mumbles
36	☐ Show-off	☐ Stubborn	☐ Skeptical	☐ Slow
37	☐ Loud	☐ Lord over others	☐ Loner	☐ Lazy
38	☐ Scatterbrained	☐ Short-tempered	☐ Suspicious	☐ Sluggish
39	☐ Restless	☐ Rash	☐ Revengeful	☐ Reluctant
40	☐ Changeable	☐ Crafty	☐ Critical	☐ Compromising
	_____	_____	_____	_____

SUBTOTAL: WEAKNESSES

Popular Sanguine	Powerful Choleric	Perfect Melancholy	Peaceful Phlegmatic
_____	_____	_____	_____

COMBINED TOTALS

"If you have any encouragement
from being united with Christ, if
any comfort from His love, if any
fellowship with the Spirit, if any
tenderness and compassion, then
make my joy complete by being
like-minded, having the same love,
being one in spirit and purpose.
Do nothing out of selfish ambition or
vain conceit, but in humility consider
others better than yourselves. Each
of you should look not only to
your own interests, but also to the
interests of others."

(PHILIPPIANS 2:1-4)

As you complete this book, I hope you feel like you and your spouse are finally connecting. Congratulations! However, heed this advice: keep keeping on. Your differences can be minimized, compensated, and downplayed, but will always be there under the surface. Continue in the faith, believing God stands ready to supply the wisdom, patience, and compassion needed for each and every situation. I will be praying for you, "being confident of this, that He who began a good work in you will carry it onto completion until the day of Christ Jesus." (PHILIPPIANS 1:6)

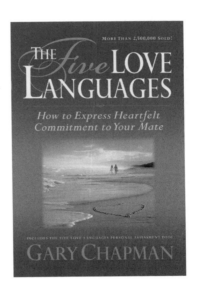